KU-487-097

JUDY RIDGWAY

BARBECUES

WARD LOCK LIMITED · LONDON

© Judy Ridgway 1983

First published in Great Britain in 1983
by Ward Lock Limited, 82 Gower Street,
London WC1E 6EQ, a Pentos Company.

Reprinted 1983

All Rights Reserved. No part of this publication
may be reproduced, stored in a retrieval system,
or transmitted, in any form or by any means,
electronic, mechanical, photocopying, recording,
or otherwise, without the prior permission of the
Copyright owners.

Text filmset in 10/11 pt Goudy Old Style
by HBM Typesetting, Chorley, Lancs.
Printed and bound in Italy by Sagdos SpA

British Library Cataloguing in Publication Data

Ridgway, Judy
   Barbecues
   1. Barbecue cookery
   I. Title
   641.7'58   TX840.B3

   ISBN 0-7063-6248-9

Acknowledgements
Cover photograph by David Johnson
Inside photography by Edmund Goldspink
Photographs on pages 8–9, page 37 and page 41 supplied
courtesy of Frank Odell Limited, New Zealand Lamb
Information Bureau and Alcan Polyfoil Ltd respectively
Line drawings by Sue Sharples

The author and publishers would also like to thank Frank
Odell Limited for kindly loaning barbecue equipment for
photography, and The Craftsman Potters Association for
loaning the glazed platter on page 21.

BARBECUES

CONTENTS

Notes

It is important to follow *either* the metric *or* the imperial measures when using the recipes in this book. Do not use a combination of measures.

All recipes serve four people, unless otherwise specified.

INTRODUCTION

There is nothing quite like the smell of charcoal smoke on a summer evening. To me it spells relaxation and enjoyment. As the cook of the house the decision to have a barbecue is more than welcome, for the chances are that the major part of the cooking will be unloaded on to someone else!

Most men seem to enjoy messing about with the barbecue, children love cooking their own food and even guests do not mind having a go, thereby spreading the work-load. With such an easy evening to look forward to, I am quite happy to organize the marinating of the meat and to make a few sauces and salads.

Of course, barbecues are not limited to the evening; lunchtime barbecues are just as popular at the weekend. Sunday lunch round the barbecue brings the family together, and friends and neighbours are usually more than eager to join in and turn the gathering into a real party.

Indeed, the joy of a barbecue is its flexibility. Provided that it is not actually raining or blowing a gale, a barbecue can be pressed into service at any time – to liven up a dull day, to entertain an unexpected guest or to celebrate a child's birthday. An informal buffet party or a gala evening will take on an added glamour if the setting is a sunny patio or a starlit garden, and the barbecue, of course, provides the food.

Nor need the possession of a barbecue be tied to the possession of a garden or patio. There are a growing number of specially designated picnic areas dotted around the countryside which are specifically geared up for safe barbecuing. Some of them have a communal barbecue while others have areas in which you may set up your own equipment. There will also be benches and tables at which to eat and litter bins to take the rubbish afterwards.

So if you live in a block of flats or only have a tiny garden, put the barbecue in the back of the car and go off for a picnic in the country. Even if you do not come across a special picnic area, the barbecue can be set up on the beach or by a running stream. Just make sure that the sparks are not going to blow on to dry timber or foliage and be sure to douse the ashes with plenty of water before leaving.

Camp and caravan sites, too, often have barbecue facilities and if you are taking the car on a touring holiday, be sure to leave room for the barbecue. It will solve many an eating problem.

Some people complain that cooking on a barbecue can be an expensive business and there is no doubt that the fuel costs are going to be higher with a barbecue than with a conventional cooker. But to my mind the fun and enjoyment far outweigh any adverse cost factor.

Expenditure can, however, be kept to a minimum on a charcoal barbecue by making sure that you use only the correct amount of chips or briquettes for the job in hand, and if you have a large or permanent and much used barbecue, you might think about buying in bulk.

The food costs will, of course, depend upon what you decide to serve, but sausages, hamburgers and chicken are both inexpensive and highly popular. Serve them on their own or include them in the party mix, and the meat costs will be much lower than if you only serve steaks and chops. Kebabs, too, can be quite economical as the pieces of meat are interspersed with much cheaper vegetables.

Barbecuing is not really a new method of cooking. The word refers to the Haitian word *barbacoa* which means a grid of green twigs suspended on sticks over a fire. The South American Indians used this as their main method of cooking and they were not alone in this. The same method was developed and used many hundreds of years ago in the near East, in South East Asia and in the islands of the Pacific.

Not surprisingly with a way of cooking that has been around for so long, there is very little which cannot be cooked on a barbecue. Whether your favourite food is lobster, steak, hamburger or sausages, it can be cooked in this way.

Cooking on a barbecue is very much a hobby with lots of people and the enthusiasts all have their own special recipes for sauces, marinades and barbecue bastes. I have been collecting these favourites for some time, and this book is the result combined with some very intensive experimentation on my own part.

In making my choice I have tried to please most tastes, and sincerely hope that there will be something to interest both beginners and experts alike. So get out the equipment, round up the family or send out invitations and get the barbecue going.

My dictionary describes a barbecue as 'an open-air party at which animals are roasted whole' – I only wish I had a garden and a barbecue big enough!

Judy Ridgway

7

CHOOSING THE BARBECUE

The choice of barbecues commercially available today is extremely wide but if you cannot find one exactly to suit your needs you can always build your own (see pages 10–11).

HIBACHI-STYLE CHARCOAL BARBECUES

The simplest of the ready-made barbecues is the Hibachi style of grill. This was first developed in Japan and *hibachi* is the Japanese word for fire bowl. It is an extremely compact barbecue, eminently suited for use in the garden, for picnics and for camping and caravanning holidays. It has a solid cast iron or steel fire bowl with vents and grills and several cooking levels. Choose from two or three grill models with small squat feet for use on the ground or on a small stone or metal table; alternatively, choose a round single grill model with a centre leg and wheels.

A typical hibachi-style charcoal barbecue

PORTABLE CHARCOAL BARBECUES

Portable barbecues come in all shapes and sizes. They may have round or square metal bowls and can be large or small. They usually have three or four folding or removable legs, sometimes with wheels. Depending upon the price, they may have windshields, adjustable grill heights, spit rods with or without motors, an undershelf and a warming tray.

PORTABLE CHARCOAL BARBECUE KETTLES

This type of barbecue is rather similar to the portable model but it has a lid which can be used as a windshield or which can be closed for maximum heat reflection and flavour retention. Even large pieces of meat can be cooked without a spit since the closed barbecue kettle acts just like a conventional oven. It is available in all shapes and sizes and some models also have side tables, shelves and warming racks.

TROLLEY BARBECUES FOR CHARCOAL, GAS OR ELECTRICITY

The most sophisticated barbecues are usually mounted on four-wheel trolleys for maximum stability. They may be open or lidded and usually come with spit-roasting and kebab attachments. Some of them are charcoal-fired, but others are fuelled by gas or electricity.

The gas and electric barbecues usually work by heating reusable volcanic rock over burners. An adjustable grill shelf is positioned over the top, and any fat splash will give a similar smoky flavour to that produced over charcoal.

How to Make the Choice

The type and size of barbecue to choose depends very much on how often you plan to use it, in what context and for how many people. Obviously it is not worth investing a lot of money in a sophisticated trolley barbecue if you only plan to use it once or twice. On the other hand, a small hibachi-type of barbecue would be an excellent choice for picnics and camping holidays but would not be nearly large enough for a full scale barbecue party.

A permanent barbecue is obviously useful if you entertain often. It should be remembered, however, that a large garden will be required, and that the ideal positioning of the barbecue may not be quite where you want it. Additionally, a permanent barbecue cannot, of course, be moved.

An improvized barbecue is useful at the very outset of your barbecue career, but is restricting and not very pleasing if you are barbecuing regularly.

SIZE AND SHAPE

Start by assessing how much you are likely to use the barbecue and how it will fit into your general life-style. Next, think about the size of the grill. If you have a large family or enjoy entertaining a lot, a small grill will mean long delays. The grilling area should at least be large enough to cater for the family. Circular grills often offer larger grilling areas than rectangular ones. But remember, too, to think about the amount of space you have. Is your barbecue area large enough to take the model you like?

HEIGHT AND STABILITY

Many people prefer to be able to stand up to do the cooking and this means that a portable barbecue with legs or set on a trolley might be ideal. It also means that permanent garden barbecues should be built to a reasonable height.

When buying a barbecue with legs, always ask to see it set up so that you can check if it is at a comfortable height for cooking. Check the stability at the same time. Circular barbecues can sometimes be very much more unstable than rectangular ones, and with both kinds, see how far the legs stick out – you could trip over them.

VENTS AND DRAUGHT CONTROL

In still weather air vents in the base or sides of the fire box make little difference to the ease of lighting or to the level of the fire. However, in windy weather those with vents are much easier to operate.

Top   *Three types of portable charcoal barbecue*
Centre *Two barbecue kettles, with lids acting as windshields*
Below   *Trolley barbecues are generally fuelled by gas or electricity*

GAS, ELECTRICITY OR CHARCOAL

The big factor here is very much one of cost. The electric and gas models tend to be very much more expensive than the average charcoal barbecue. Their main attraction is in the speed with which they reach a suitable cooking temperature. There is very little waiting around. In addition some of them can be used indoors.

However, for most people, part of the fun of the barbecue rests with the smell of the charcoal wafting across the garden, and part of the general mystique includes also the general preparation involved in getting the charcoal going.

There is also some disagreement about whether or not the food has quite the same sort of 'charcoal' flavour when it has been cooked on a gas or electric barbecue. However, it is the fat that drips on to the charcoal which causes the smoke and gives the smoky taste. This process happens in just the same way on gas and electric barbecue grills as on charcoal barbecues so that the taste should be the same.

SPIT-ROASTING

Special spit-roasting and kebab attachments are very enjoyable and can widen the scope of the cooking on the barbecue. However, many of them have no locking device and this means that the food always rests with the heaviest part over the grill. The only answer is to hold it in different positions – a very hot job – or to wedge it with a heat-resistant wedge. You must also remember to keep moving it on and watching it so that the food gets cooked all the way round.

Some models have a battery-driven motor to turn the spit and these can also be bought as a separate item. If using one of these, the meat is continually turned over the coals, and, provided that the spit is inserted centrally through the joint or bird, the meat will cook evenly. There will also be a minimum of strain on the motor. There is no need to baste meat cooked on a spit as it is self-basting.

EXTRA ATTACHMENTS

Many barbecue models have a long list of optional extras such as shelving and hooks for utensils. Some of them are quite useful if you do a lot of barbecuing, but a garden table at the side of the grill will serve the same purpose.

MAKING YOUR OWN PORTABLE BARBECUE

If you are a do-it-yourself enthusiast, you may like to make your own barbecue. A simple one can be made out of a large metal bowl or an old *shallow* bucket.
1) Punch holes in the base and sides; a regular pattern looks better than random holes.
2) Stand on a base of bricks and make a grill to go over the top.

You could even press an old metal wheelbarrow into service.
1) Fill the base with stones.
2) Cover with a foil-lined grid to take the coals.
3) Finish off with an oven shelf across the top to act as the grill.

Note Always use the foil with the dull side facing the coals. This reduces the chance of the foil catching fire.

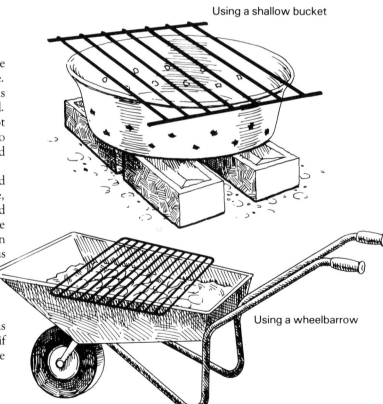

Using a shallow bucket

Using a wheelbarrow

BUILDING A PERMANENT BARBECUE

More permanent barbecues are just as easy to build. Bricks can be bought at the local builders merchant, and a very simple barbecue can be constructed as follows:

1) Lay two or three layers of bricks in two parallel rows.
2) Place a grill across the top.
3) If the barbecue is in an exposed place, it is probably sensible to fill in the back of the barbecue as well. Leave ventilation openings towards the prevailing summer wind.
4) Place a double layer of foil on the ground under the grill.
5) Cover with shingle or clean gravel to a depth of 5mm–1.25cm/¼–½ inch.
6) Lay the charcoal on top of this.

Properly laid bricks will be a safer proposition for a family or for barbecues which are likely to be used by guests. Start by choosing a really level piece of ground, possibly covered with concrete, tiles or flagstones.

1) Measure out the size of cooking space required.
2) Lay the bricks on three sides of the area, leaving one of the long sides open.
3) Build the rows to a height of four bricks and then lay the grate. This could take the form of a row of 1.25cm/½ inch metal bars set about 2.5–3.75cm/1–1½ inches apart and fixed in with mortar.
4) Continue with two more rows of bricks.
5) Set in the grid. This might be more bars, chicken wire or an oven shelf. If you are using chicken wire, you will need to have some loose bricks to lay on top.

Other designs use a large slab of real stone or slate where the bars are above. A fire basket is then placed on the slab. Avoid concrete or reconstructed stone as the heat could cause it to explode, and do not light the fire directly on the slab or it will crack.

Make sure that the mortar on a permanent barbecue is properly dried out before you use the barbecue. Cover it with wet sacks for the first week after laying; then uncover and dry out for another week before lighting up.

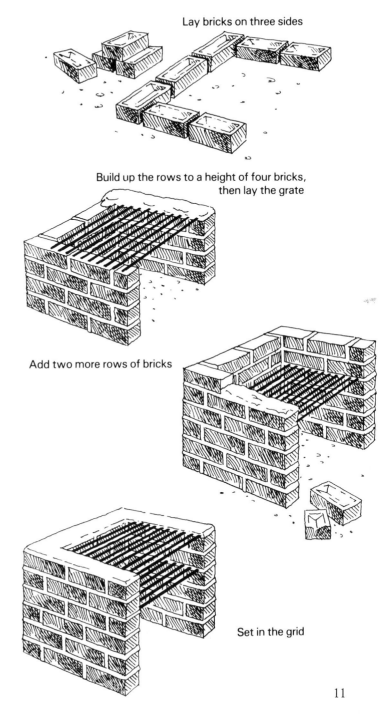

Lay bricks on three sides

Build up the rows to a height of four bricks, then lay the grate

Add two more rows of bricks

Set in the grid

BARBECUE KNOW-HOW

Careful siting of the barbecue is the first step to safe and successful parties. If you are planning a permanent barbecue you will not want to move it again, so think very carefully before you start building. Is the proposed site too near to the house? Will it disturb the neighbours? Is there a source of gas or water nearby?

Check the prevailing wind in the area and take this into account too. Remember that some smoke and cooking smells are inevitable and that the people next door will not want to be continually reminded of your new toy. Easy access to the barbecue is another factor to bear in mind, particularly if you plan to entertain outdoors regularly.

Portable barbecues are more flexible and can be sited according to the wind direction on the day, but you must still take safety and nuisance factors into account.

Make sure that the barbecue is not sited too close to any fences or trellis work and that it is standing on a firm and level base. In really hot summers it is much safer to stand the barbecue on concrete or flagstones, well away from dry bushes or undergrowth. See that you have plenty of water around to extinguish any sparks which look like smouldering.

Never site a charcoal barbecue inside the house or in any kind of enclosed space. The charcoal gives off carbon monoxide gas which is highly poisonous.

Fuels and Equipment

Although an *electric* barbecue is simply plugged into a socket, the barbecue will need to be sited near to such a point or a long flex will be needed. In either case, the flex should be well marked so that there is no chance of anyone tripping over it. If the flex crosses a terrace or footpath, it is a good idea to cover it with a piece of carpet or an old rug.

Gas barbecues can be run on bottled propane or butane gas or on natural gas. The bottled gas will usually last for quite a number of barbecues. When it runs out, the containers are quite simply replaced. They can be obtained from hardware stores. Natural gas barbecues can be plumbed into the gas mains running to a permanent site or attached to a long flexible hose.

Gas pokers can be used for starting up charcoal barbecues. You will need to have a long hose or to have the poker converted to run off a camping gas cylinder.

Charcoal for barbecues comes in different forms, as follows:

Charcoal chips can be made from traditional pure hardwood charcoal or they can be treated for easy lighting. Traditional chips will need the addition of kindling or lighter fluid, and will be ready for cooking within 15–20 minutes; treated chips will be ready for cooking within 10 minutes.

Charcoal can also be bought in compressed briquette form. These are more difficult to light than chips but they will burn for very much longer and are therefore much more economical.

However, if you just want to barbecue steaks for four people, then there are packs of small square charcoal briquettes. These are instant burning so that barbecuing can start within 15 minutes.

Charcoal can be bought from most departmental stores, ironmongers, garden centres, coal merchants and some supermarkets. Store it in the bag in which it comes and make sure that it does not get damp.

Wood is not advisable as a fuel. It flares up, burns out too quickly, and there may be fumes resulting from the resin.

As a starter, you will need to apply a little help in the form of some kind of kindling or starter fuel to most charcoal products. Rolled up newspapers and dry sticks should be sufficient to get charcoal chips alight but for briquettes you will need to use one of the following:

Starter or lighter fluid: Soak the briquettes in the fluid for a few hours before lighting the barbecue or sprinkle carefully over the coals when they are arranged in the fire box.

Methylated spirits: Sprinkle over the coals when they are arranged in the fire box. Do not use too much.

Lighter paste: Simply squeeze the paste in amongst the coals as you build them up at the start.

Solid fuel tablets and non-chemical firelighters: These are usually specially formulated for barbecue use. Break up large blocks and mix with the briquettes in the fire box.

Avoid using highly inflammable items like paraffin, petrol or alcohol; they are dangerous and taint the food.

Other equipment: Useful items include a long poker for moving the coals around and a heatproof glove or gauntlet to enable you to get close enough to deal with difficult coals.

Lighting Up A Charcoal Barbecue

The quantity of charcoal required depends upon the amount of food you have to cook and the size of your grill. The general aim is to provide a good even heat throughout the coals but this does not mean that you have to use a lot of charcoal. In fact, you will probably get better results if you use the charcoal sparingly thereby benefiting your pocket also.

Some of the charcoal chips come in measured amounts, with accompanying instructions. As a general guide to briquettes, you will need 16–20 compressed charcoal nuggets for a small square grill, and 25–30 for a larger circular barbecue.

STEP-BY-STEP GUIDE TO STARTING UP A CHARCOAL BARBECUE

1) Place the grill, if it is portable, in a reasonably sheltered place.
2) Set the ventilator flaps, if there are any, to the half-open position, varying the vent size to the wind conditions.
3) Place the kindling, if used, in the base of the fire bowl, arranging the charcoal on the top. Otherwise, mix solid fire lighters with the charcoal, or sprinkle liquid starters over the top.
4) Gather the coals up into a pyramid shape; this helps the air to circulate. Use two pyramids if the barbecue is large. Put a match to the kindling, solid fire lighters or the soaked or sprinkled briquettes. Initially, the flames will flare up, then gradually die down. A portable barbecue may then be turned into the breeze and the vents opened fully.
5) After about 10–15 minutes the edges of the charcoal will have turned grey and this colour will gradually spread all over the coals. As the fire takes hold, spread the coals so that they cover the whole of the base of the barbecue. Do not separate them during this spreading-out process.
6) If the coals do not quite cover the base, add one or two new ones to fill in the gaps. Once the coals are hot enough to start cooking, the vents can be closed for longer slower burning.

Judging the Coals

The fire will be ready for cooking when the coals are grey all over. At night they will start to produce a soft red glow. Do not start to cook too soon for the coals will just not be hot enough, the fatty drips could smother the coals which are starting to burn and the starter solids or fluids may not be fully burnt off.

If you are not quite sure that the coals are ready, try the hand test. Hold your hand, palm towards the heat, at about grill level. If you have to withdraw your hand in about 4–5 seconds, this means that the coals are low, in 3–4 seconds, that they are medium, in 3 seconds, that they are hot.

SHUTTING DOWN THE BARBECUE

Once you have finished cooking, the charcoal can be left to burn out. However, if you have misjudged the quantities, this could be rather a waste. Douse the coals with plenty of water, leave them to dry in the sun and use again as required. Burnt out coals can also be extinguished with earth.

Maintaining and Storing the Barbecue

Very many barbecue grills are chrome plated and if they are looked after, will last for quite a long time. Do not place the grill on the fire until ready to use and do not leave it on the fire after the cooking is finished. If possible, place the grill in hot water while still hot and use a non-abrasive scourer for cleaning.

Special grill brushes, scrapers and cleaning spray can be bought to help keep your barbecue in peak condition.

Always wipe out the rest of the barbecue to remove any grease, and clear out all the ashes on a charcoal barbecue.

To clean a gas barbecue, close the lid, turn the gas full on for 10–15 minutes, and leave until the fat has come off the lower rack.

If you have a portable barbecue, store it indoors to prevent rusting. Cover permanent barbecues with heavy-duty polythene and remove any metal parts. Scrape down and clean the grid as frequently as possible.

When storing a portable barbecue for the winter, place a light film of petroleum jelly over all the chrome or bright and moving parts; this helps to protect them from rust and from seizing up.

JOIN US FOR A BARBECUE PARTY

However appealing it is to eat out of doors and particularly to barbecue food, do not get too carried away. A tiny barbecue and a small terrace garden will soon be overcrowded, and even if you have space for all your guests, the last to be served will not be too pleased if they have had to wait for the sixth or seventh batch of hamburgers.

Tailor your numbers to fit the available space and the size of the barbecue. Small parties can be just as much fun as large ones. However, if you do have a large barbecue or can loan one or two from friends, you can really be extravagant.

In either case, success will depend on how good your planning has been. Sit down in advance and make a check-list (see opposite), decide whether the guests are to cook for themselves or whether you will be batch-cooking for them. A large permanent barbecue with easy access is ideal for guests to cook for themselves. Set up a raw food buffet at the side with plenty of oil, bastes and sauces, and let everyone help themselves. Large trolley barbecues also lend themselves to this method of cooking.

Portable barbecues, however, usually mean a single or possibly two chefs. They are not always very stable and a lot of people all using them at once could lead to a disaster. Here the buffet will be better set up with starters, salads, sauces and the barbecued items as they are cooked.

Will it be a lunchtime or evening barbecue? Candles or hired lighting create instant atmosphere at night, together with lighting from inside the house. It is also important that the barbecue and buffet area are well lit, particularly if everyone is cooking their own food.

Planning must also include contingency planning. What will you do if it rains? It is often quite possible to continue with the barbecue in a sheltered spot and bring the food into the house to be eaten. Otherwise, the food will all have to be cooked in the oven or under a conventional grill.

Safety cannot be over-emphasized. Always wear gauntlets, keep long hair away from the heat, and do not wear full sleeves. Site the barbecue away from any obvious danger such as fences, wood, tablecloths, and anything inflammable such as petrol and chemicals. Do not trail long flexes.

CHOOSING AND PREPARING THE FOOD

The menu for a barbecue should centre on the barbecue itself with a choice perhaps of chops, kebabs and hamburgers, or a spit-roast with sausages and barbecued vegetables, plus barbecued desserts which use up the last heat. Choose one or two simple starters to ward off hunger pangs as the food is cooking, and add a couple of desserts to finish. The rest of the food will be designed to go with the barbecued items and could include rice and potato dishes, salads, bread, a good choice of sauces, relishes and chutneys, and some non-barbecued desserts also.

Prepare and cook as much food as you can in advance, leaving only the salads to be tossed, the bread to be warmed and the main dish to be cooked over the barbecue. If you are having a large party, choose starters and desserts which can be prepared earlier in the week and stored in a refrigerator or freezer. Prepare the meat the day before, marinate in a refrigerator overnight and finish off as much as possible before your guests arrive.

SITING OF BARBECUE, BUFFET AND SEATING ARRANGEMENTS

Give some thought, too, to the siting of the barbecue and buffet. If everyone is to cook their own food, the raw food buffet will need to be near to the barbecue. Starters, salads and other accompaniments and desserts may then be set out on another table further away from the barbecue. This avoids too much congestion round the cooking area.

This is equally important if there are to be only one or two chefs, and the same sort of arrangements will apply though you may be able to manage with a smaller table to cook from. You will also need a table from which to serve the drinks, though if space is at a premium, these could be dispensed from the house.

Barbecues are usually very informal, but it, nevertheless, is difficult to eat and drink standing up, so that it is important to use all your garden furniture and to bring out any chairs from the house which will not be harmed by sinking into the lawn. Cushions and rugs can also be put into service.

SERVING THE FOOD

Make sure that there are plenty of plates and eating utensils. With this kind of running buffet, guests tend to put their plates down between eating different items from the barbecue and then pick up new ones. It is well worth considering the use of plastic or paper plates and plastic utensils. But even if you do not want to go this far, it is probably better not to use your best china service.

Make the buffet look as attractive as possible, perhaps with a gaily covered paper tablecloth and matching napkins. Flowers, too, always look pretty on a buffet. Remember to label everything – not everyone likes chilli sauce or mustard – and put out plenty of serving utensils.

CHILDREN'S BARBECUE PARTIES

Barbecue parties where children will be present represent even more of a safety hazard, and some thought should be given to cordoning off the barbecue area. It is one thing to let your own children cook on the barbecue when you are alone with plenty of time to supervize them, but quite another to allow other people's children to use it when they may be virtually unsupervized.

If the party is to be specifically a children's party, the menu will need some adjustment. Quickly cooked items will overcome the boredom of waiting around for the food and, luckily, foods like hamburgers and sausages combine speed of cooking with popularity among the young age groups! Even so, a few games, perhaps hunting for clues and presents around the garden, will help to keep the children occupied while the barbecue gets going.

Do make an effort to find the right kind of sesame buns for hamburgers and long rolls for hotdog sausages. Children will appreciate the *real* thing much more than their parents who would probably prefer your own home-cooked rolls. Young people's tastes are very conservative – a philosophy of 'baked beans with everything' will go a long way to ensure success.

When the food is cooked, it is a good idea to join the chef to help with the serving out. Buffets are not a good idea with children. Huge helpings of tomato ketchup will take the place of even a token serving of salad and their parents will not thank you if they are kept up half the night!

CHECK-LIST FOR A BARBECUE PARTY

Fix the date and invite the guests
Plan the menu
Prepare shopping lists for advance preparation and on the day
Check stocks of charcoal and starter fuel or gas cylinders
Prepare those dishes which can be made in advance, eg starters and desserts
Prepare sauces and marinades and leave meat or fish to stand in a cool place
Site and set up the barbecue buffet and drinks tables
Check that all cooking equipment and utensils are handy
Write labels for meat, sauces and relishes and instructions for cooking if required
Prepare remaining dishes, eg salads and fillers
Finish off buffet table and check cutlery and crockery
Organize seating, lighting, disposal bins, etc
Set up the barbecue
Bring out all the food

COOKING ON A BARBECUE

Although barbecue cooking is very simple, it is quite different from cooking in a conventional manner. The food is cooked directly over the heat source, and if care is not exercized, flare ups from dripping fat can result in burnt offerings rather than succulent steaks. On the other hand, the meat does need to be kept moist, so that basting is important.

The barbecue gives off a good deal of heat, so that special long-handled equipment will be needed to handle the food. This heat also means that the food will be cooked relatively quickly. The meat must be as tender as possible to start with and this often means marinating it beforehand.

Different kinds of food will require different methods of preparation and cooking, and these are covered in the introductions to the recipe chapters. The following is a general guide to cooking on a barbecue.

CHECK-LIST OF COOKING EQUIPMENT

Oven gloves or gauntlets
Long-handled fork, spoon and fish slice
Large sharp knife and chopping board
At least one pair of long tongs
Skewers
Hinged wire grills for food which may break up during cooking
Perforated spoon for removing meat from marinades
Brushes for basting
Aluminium foil
Paper napkins and kitchen paper
Meat thermometer

FLAME DOUSERS

The important thing when barbecuing is to have heat and not flames. Some flare ups are unavoidable and so you will need to have some means of dousing the flames without reducing the heat. Any of the following items can be pressed into service:

Well washed squeezy washing-up liquid bottle
Flour dredger
Water pistol
Plastic plant spray
Large rhubarb or cabbage leaves

AROMATIC SMOKE

A handful of fresh herbs or specially prepared aromatic wood chips sprinkled over the coals just before cooking not only fills the air with their delicious aroma but also penetrates the meat whilst it is cooking.

Pick the herbs fresh from your herb garden or buy them at the greengrocer on the day of the barbecue. Choose rosemary, marjoram, thyme or oregano for a really aromatic result. Use bay leaves or fennel stalks for fish. Alternatively, you can buy hickory chips at your barbecue supplier; these need to be soaked in water before use, or you could try apple or cherry twigs.

GENERAL STEP-BY-STEP GUIDE TO GRILLING

1) Bring the coals to the required heat as outlined on page 13. Sprinkle with herbs or hickory, if using. Switch on gas or electric barbecue.

2) Lightly oil the grill and place on the barbecue. Pieces of bacon rind or fat trimmed from the meat can be used up here.

3) Brush the kebabs, hamburgers, chops or steaks with oil or melted butter, season to taste and place the oiled side on the grid. Do not overcrowd the grill as this causes too much drip and, therefore, excessive smoke.

4) Cook on one side for as long as indicated by the recipe. Brush the second side with fat, turn over and continue cooking.

5) If a baste or glaze is to be used, start to brush on towards the end of the cooking time. This is particularly important with glazes containing jam, sugar or tomato ketchup as these will soon start to burn, and, instead of imparting a good flavour to the food, will simply make it taste nasty.

6) Watch all food, basted or unbasted, while it is cooking to ensure that it does not burn, and start testing to see if it is cooked a short while before the final cooking time given in the recipe.
7) Take care when lifting the lid on a barbecue kettle. All the hot air and steam will rush out at once and could cause burns.
8) Wipe the grill over between each batch of food, and brush with oil again before resuming cooking.

GENERAL STEP-BY-STEP GUIDE TO SPIT-ROASTING

1) Prepare and marinate the joint if necessary, overnight.
2) Arrange and light the coals. Always use plenty of charcoal when roasting a large joint. You do not want the heat to run down before the joint is cooked. A 2–2.5kg/4–5 lb roast will require about 2.5kg/5 lb of charcoal to cook. Beef and lamb may be served pink, but pork and poultry should be thoroughly cooked through. The best way to make sure that the meat is cooked sufficiently is to use a meat thermometer.
3) Use a drip tray to catch the drips. This can be a ready-made foil tray, or can be improvized by folding and shaping a piece of double-thickness foil round a book. Arrange the foil so that the shiny side faces in and the dull side out. Hold the corners together with paper clips. Place the tray on the coals under the joint; this will prevent fat from flaring up on the fire. Vegetables can be cooked in the drip tray towards the end of the cooking time.
4) Place the joint on the spit right in the centre.
5) Lightly grease the joint if it has not been marinated in an oil-based marinade.
6) Glaze or baste the joint during the last 20 minutes of cooking time.

COOKING IN FOIL

Some delicate foods such as fish benefit from being cooked in foil parcels. The fish can be kept moist and the foil parcel will help to stop it falling apart. Extra flavourings can be added to the parcel to vary the taste.

Lamb and pork chops are also very good cooked in this way. Vegetables, too, take well to the foil parcel method. Wrap with the dull side of the foil on the outside.

Foil parcels are usually placed on the grill and turned once during the cooking time. However, potatoes can be wrapped in foil and placed in the embers to cook, thereby making maximum use of all the available heat. The length of time taken to cook will depend upon the size of the potatoes.

SMOKE COOKING

Covered barbecues have this additional facility. The food is placed on the grill or spit and covered with the lid which acts like an oven. It is suitable for large joints, especially those that are to be spit-roasted, as it reduces the total cooking time.

SMOKE BOX

This is useful for cooking fish so as to give it a smoky flavour. Sawdust or woodchip is used in the box.

REGULATING THE HEAT

Whatever method of cooking you are using, you may want to regulate the heat. This is quite simple, of course, with the gas and electric barbecues where heat control is just a matter of turning a knob. Charcoal, however, is not quite so easy to regulate. The following methods are a guideline:

To increase the heat:
Lower the grill nearer to the coals
Open the vents to increase the draught, but remember that the charcoal will burn out more quickly
Move the coals closer together and add more charcoal at the sides of the burning coals, not on top

To reduce the heat:
Move the grill further away from the coals
Spread the coals out
Make a circular well in the coals to decentralize the heat

WHILE YOU WAIT

Cold dishes are the most suitable choice for starters as they can usually be made in advance. They can be arranged on the buffet prior to your guests' arrival and handed round as required. Remember to choose dishes which are easy to eat with the fingers, a fork or a spoon.

If you are cooking for more than four people, double up on the quantities or serve a selection of dips or starters.

SMOKED CLAM DIP

100g/4oz canned smoked clams
175g/6oz curd cheese
juice of ½ lemon
3–4 cocktail gherkins, very finely chopped
black pepper
2×15ml spoons/2 tablespoons milk

Mince the clams and mix with the remaining ingredients or process in a blender or food processor, adding enough milk to give a creamy consistency.

Serve with carrot, cucumber and celery sticks as dippers.

AUBERGINE AND GARLIC DIP

1 medium-sized aubergine (375g/12oz)
1–2 cloves garlic, crushed
½ small onion, chopped **or** grated
juice of ½ lemon
salt, black pepper
1×15ml spoon/1 tablespoon olive oil
2–3 black olives
sprigs parsley
paprika

Place the whole unpeeled aubergine under the grill and cook for about 20–30 minutes, turning from time to time. Leave to cool a little and then cut the aubergine in half lengthways. Scoop out the flesh, and process in a blender or food processor with the garlic, onion and lemon juice. Alternatively, sieve the flesh and mix with garlic, *grated* onion and lemon juice. Season to taste. Just before serving, stir in the olive oil, and garnish with black olives and sprigs of parsley. Sprinkle with paprika.

Use strips of toasted pitta bread as dippers.

VIRGINIA SPINACH DIP

250g/8oz frozen chopped spinach, thawed
3×15ml spoons/3 tablespoons freshly chopped parsley
50g/2oz Virginia ham, very finely chopped
4–5×15ml spoons/4–5 tablespoons mayonnaise
salt, pepper

Drain the spinach very well by pressing against the sides of a sieve. Turn into a basin and mix in the remaining ingredients, seasoning to taste. Add a little more mayonnaise if the mixture is too thick.

Serve with potato crisps as dippers.

SMOKED MACKEREL DIP

100g/4oz smoked mackerel fillet
175g/6oz curd cheese
juice of ½ lemon
3–4 cocktail gherkins, very finely chopped
black pepper
2×15ml spoons/2 tablespoons milk

Remove any skin and bone from the mackerel fillet and mash with a fork. Mix with all the remaining ingredients, apart from the milk, or process in a blender or food processor, adding enough milk to give a creamy consistency.

Serve with carrot, cucumber and celery sticks as dippers.

CHEESE AND ASPARAGUS DIP

300g/10oz canned asparagus tips
100g/4oz cream cheese
salt, pepper

Sieve the asparagus tips and mix with the cream cheese, or process together in a blender or food processor. Season to taste.

Serve with vegetable crudités or potato crisps as dippers.

GUACAMOLE

2 ripe avocado pears, peeled and stoned
juice of 1 lemon **or** lime
1 small onion, very finely chopped
1 clove of garlic, crushed
1 fresh green chilli, de-seeded and very finely chopped
1×15ml spoon/1 tablespoon freshly chopped parsley
1×5ml spoon/1 teaspoon olive oil
salt, black pepper
a pinch of Cayenne pepper

Sieve the avocados with the lemon or lime juice, or purée in a blender. Stir in all the remaining ingredients, and spoon into a bowl.

Serve with green pepper and carrot sticks and cauliflower florets as dippers.

PARSLEY CHEESE BALLS

For an attractive platter, serve mixed with American Prawn Balls. The quantities given assume that they will be served together. If you are catering for a party, make up further batches with other well-flavoured cheeses, such as Windsor Red, Charnwood or Ilchester.

100g/4oz Cotswold cheese, grated
2×5ml spoons/2 teaspoons any relish
4–5×15ml spoons/4–5 tablespoons freshly chopped parsley

Mix the grated cheese and relish to make a thick paste. Place the chopped parsley on a flat plate. Form the cheese mixture into 10–12 small balls. Roll in the chopped parsley, making sure that they are well coated. Place on the serving dish, and spear with cocktail sticks.

AMERICAN PRAWN BALLS

100g/4oz peeled prawns
50g/2oz cream cheese
1×5ml spoon/1 teaspoon lemon juice
salt, black pepper
50g/2oz walnuts, very finely chopped

Chop the prawns finely, then mix in the cream cheese and lemon juice. Season to taste. Place the chopped nuts on a flat plate. Shape the prawn mixture into 16 small balls, then roll in the chopped nuts, making sure that they are well coated. Place on the serving dish, and spear with cocktail sticks.

STUFFED VEGETABLE PLATTER

4 small tomatoes
150g/5oz canned sardines in tomato sauce
salt, pepper
sprigs parsley
50g/2oz liver sausage
50g/2oz curd cheese
1 green pepper, de-seeded and cut into quarters
stuffed olives, sliced
5cm/2 inches cucumber, cut into 8 slices
1 hard-boiled egg, sliced
2×5ml spoons/2 teaspoons capers
4 sticks celery
50ml/2floz soured cream
50g/2oz lumpfish roe

Cut the tomatoes in half. Scoop out and discard the centres and seeds. Mash the sardines with salt and pepper, and use to fill the tomato halves. Garnish with sprigs of parsley and arrange on a large serving plate.

Mix the liver sausage and curd cheese, and season to taste. Cut the pepper quarters in half. Spread a little of the mixture on each piece of pepper, and garnish with a stuffed olive slice. Add to the serving plate with the stuffed tomatoes.

Place the cucumber slices on the same plate and top each one with a slice of hard-boiled egg and a few capers.

Cut the sticks of celery into short lengths and fill each one with a little soured cream and a portion of lumpfish roe. Add to the serving dish with the other vegetables.

An Assortment of Starters
Parsley Cheese Balls, American Prawn Balls, Stuffed Vegetable Platter and *Aubergine and Garlic Dip (page 18)*

BACON TITBITS

Make up a single batch of titbits for four. Alternatively, double or treble the quantity of bacon and add the other batches of fillings for a barbecue party.

10 rashers streaky bacon, without rinds (175g/6oz)

FILLINGS
150g/5oz canned water chestnuts, drained
75g/3oz chicken livers, lightly sautéed and cut into pieces
or
2 rings fresh **or** canned pineapple, cut into 6 pieces each
250g/8oz canned lychees, stoned
or
12 spring onion bulbs
50g/2oz cheese, cut into 16 cubes

Grill the bacon and cut each rasher into two or three pieces. Wrap each piece round one of the fillings while still hot, and secure with a cocktail stick.

Variation
Use quartered fresh peaches, apricot halves or cubed bananas as alternatives to the fruit filling.

ORANGE, LEMON AND GRAPEFRUIT COCKTAILS

Serve a selection of these cocktails at a barbecue party or pick just one as a starter for four people.

ORANGE COCKTAIL
2 large oranges, halved
50g/2oz streaky bacon, crisply grilled and diced
2 sticks celery, finely chopped
5–6 sprigs watercress, chopped
1 × 15ml spoon / 1 tablespoon soured cream
salt, black pepper

Cut or scoop out the flesh from the orange halves. Remove any pips and thick membranes and chop the flesh. Mix with the remaining ingredients and pile back into the empty orange skins.

LEMON COCKTAIL
2 large lemons, halved
100g/4oz peeled prawns
4 spring onions, finely chopped
3.75cm/1½ inches cucumber, finely chopped
3.75cm/1½ inch slice fresh root ginger, grated
1 × 5ml spoon / 1 teaspoon soy sauce
salt, black pepper
1 × 15ml spoon / 1 tablespoon mayonnaise
1 × 5ml spoon / 1 teaspoon concentrated tomato purée
sprigs parsley

Squeeze the lemons, retaining the juice, and scrape out the remains of the flesh. Cut a slice off the base so that the hollowed skin will sit on a plate without falling over. Mix together the prawns, onions, cucumber, ginger, soy sauce and salt and pepper. Pile back into the empty shells. Mix the mayonnaise and tomato purée, and pour this over the lemons. Garnish with parsley.

GRAPEFRUIT COCKTAIL

1 large grapefruit
50g/2oz smoked ham, diced
½ small green pepper, de-seeded and finely chopped
1×15ml spoon/1 tablespoon thick mayonnaise
salt, black pepper
sprigs mint

Cut the grapefruit into four quarters lengthways. Cut the flesh away from the skins and place the empty skins on a serving plate. Remove any pith, pips or thick membranes, and chop the flesh finely. Mix with the ham, green pepper and mayonnaise, and season to taste. Pile back on to the grapefruit skins and garnish with sprigs of mint.

STUFFED EGG PLATTER

8 eggs, hard-boiled and halved
25g/1oz minced prawns
2×5ml spoons/2 teaspoons soured cream
salt, pepper
4 whole prawns
1×2.5ml spoon/½ teaspoon curry powder
4×5ml spoons/4 teaspoons mayonnaise
4 sprigs parsley
1 bunch watercress
25g/1oz minced ham
2×5ml spoons/2 teaspoons made mustard

Remove the yolks from two of the eggs and mash in a cup with the minced prawns and soured cream. Season to taste and pile back into the four half whites. Decorate with whole prawns and place on a large serving dish. Take the yolks of two more eggs and mash with curry powder and 2×5ml spoons/2 teaspoons mayonnaise. Pile back into the whites and decorate with sprigs of parsley. Arrange on the serving plate with the others.
Very finely chop 4–6 sprigs of watercress from the bunch and mash with two further egg yolks and the rest of the mayonnaise.

Season to taste and pile back into the egg whites. Add to the serving dish. Mash the remaining egg yolks with most of the ham and the mustard. Season to taste and pile back into the whites. Decorate with the rest of the minced ham and add to the platter. Garnish with the remaining watercress.

MARINATED MUSHROOM POTS

1 small onion, finely sliced
½×2.5ml spoon/¼ teaspoon fennel seeds
1×15ml spoon/1 tablespoon cooking oil
375g/12oz button mushrooms
½×2.5ml spoon/¼ teaspoon mixed herbs
a pinch of cinnamon
salt, freshly ground black pepper
1×5ml spoon/1 teaspoon concentrated tomato purée
1×2.5ml spoon/½ teaspoon Worcestershire sauce
450ml/¾ pint dry white wine **or** cider

Gently fry the onion and fennel seeds in cooking oil. Remove the stalks from the mushrooms, and chop very finely. Add to the pan with the herbs, cinnamon and seasoning. Continue frying gently until the onions are softened. Add the remaining ingredients except the mushroom caps, and bring to the boil. Cook for 5 minutes, add the mushrooms and reduce the heat. Leave to cool. Chill in a refrigerator before serving in individual ramekin dishes.
Serve with Garlic or Herb and Lemon Bread (page 70), or with wholemeal rolls.

PIQUANT POULTRY

All kinds of poultry take well to barbecue cooking. They can be jointed, marinated and grilled, split and grilled whole, or, if they are not too large, spit-roasted whole. Fresh or frozen birds can be used but do make sure that frozen birds are properly thawed out before cooking. Follow the instructions on the bag. Poultry can be thawed in your chosen marinade.

Basic Preparation and Cooking

For all methods of cooking, trim off any excess skin and fat but leave the main body of the skin intact; it will go deliciously crispy with cooking. The next step is to marinate the bird. This should be done at least 2 hours before use, ideally overnight. However, most poultry is tender enough and this may be omitted if time is short. Instead, brush with oil or butter, and season all over.

To grill, place the portions, bony side down, over the coals. The bones help to conduct the heat to the flesh. Cook for a quarter of the full cooking time and then turn over. Cook for the same amount of time. Turn twice again to complete the sequence. Remember to baste with oil or butter often, as poultry soon dries up if left over the barbecue unbasted. Sauces should not be used for basting until after the half-way mark.

Whole chickens can also be grilled. Simply split the chicken along the backbone and open out. Treat in just the same way as the joints but cook for a little longer (see cooking chart below).

Whole turkeys are too large to split and grill on most barbecues, but the bird can be jointed and cut into pieces. Slice legs along their length and open out to make butterfly joints.

Duck is a very fatty bird and it is best to pre-cook the bird in the oven before jointing, marinating and finishing off on the barbecue. Remember to prick the skin before cooking the duck to allow the fat to escape.

Spit-roasting is just as simple. Have the bird cleaned and trussed and make sure that the legs and wings will be kept close to the body. Use extra skewers where necessary and either cut off the neck skin or skewer if flat. Drive the spit in from a point just in front of the parson's nose and bring it out around the top of the wishbone. Remember to ensure that the bird is evenly balanced or it will strain the rôtisserie motor. Baste the bird with a sauce or any remaining marinade towards the end of the cooking time.

Whole turkeys will be too large and heavy for most rôtisseries but joints work well or you could try one of the ready-prepared turkey joints which are available. Pre-cook duck before spit-roasting.

It is very important to ensure that poultry is properly cooked. To test if it is really cooked through, pierce the thickest part of the meat with a sharp knife or skewer, and push right through to the bone. The juice should be quite clear with no tinge of pink.

CHART OF COOKING TIMES

Bird	grill	spit-roast
chicken and turkey breast (boned)	15–20 minutes	–
chicken and small turkey joints	20–30 minutes	–
whole split chicken	30–40 minutes	–
whole chicken	–	2–3 hours (less with a barbecue kettle)
duck joints (pre-cooked)	10–15 minutes	–
whole duck (pre-cooked)	–	30–40 minutes

Marinated chicken awaiting barbecuing and basting

Marinades and Bastes

Chicken easily takes up the flavour of marinades and bastes, and so they should not be too strong. On the other hand, turkey, particularly the leg meat, and duck have much stronger flavours of their own and can withstand a more robust marinade.

The following are a few to choose from. Remember, too, that most of the sauces given on pages 65–6 can also be used for basting.

HERB AND YOGHURT MARINADE FOR CHICKEN

150g/5oz natural yoghurt
1×5ml spoon/1 teaspoon lemon juice
1 clove of garlic, crushed
1×15ml spoon/1 tablespoon freshly chopped parsley
1×5ml spoon/1 teaspoon dried mixed herbs
$\frac{1}{2}$×2.5ml spoon/$\frac{1}{4}$ teaspoon dried rosemary, tarragon **or** basil
a pinch of nutmeg **or** mace

Place all the ingredients in a bowl, and mix well together. Dry the chicken or chicken joints and place in the marinade, spooning some of the mixture all over the chicken. Cover and leave to stand in a cool place for at least 2 hours.

Note Use also to baste chicken.

SPICY MARINADE FOR TURKEY

100g/4oz clear honey
2×15ml spoons/2 tablespoons tomato ketchup
2×15ml spoons/2 tablespoons soy sauce
2×15ml spoons/2 tablespoons malt vinegar
1×15ml spoon/1 tablespoon Worcestershire sauce
1×5ml spoon/1 teaspoon ground ginger
1×2.5ml spoon/$\frac{1}{2}$ teaspoon mixed herbs
3–4 drops Tabasco sauce

Mix all the ingredients together in a bowl, stirring until all the honey has dissolved. Place the turkey joints or pieces in the marinade and leave to stand in a cool place for a few hours or, if possible, overnight. Turn the meat in the marinade from time to time.

QUICK BARBECUE BASTE FOR ANY POULTRY

1×15ml spoon/1 tablespoon dry mustard
1×15ml spoon/1 tablespoon cornflour
300ml/$\frac{1}{2}$ pint chicken stock
4×15ml spoons/4 tablespoons tomato ketchup
2×15ml spoons/2 tablespoons Worcestershire sauce
50g/2oz brown sugar
salt, paprika

Mix the mustard and cornflour, and gradually blend in the stock. Add all the other ingredients, pour into a pan and bring to the boil, stirring all the time. Simmer for a few minutes and use to baste the meat towards the end of the cooking time. Re-heat any remaining baste and serve as a sauce with the cooked meat.

PROVENÇALE BASTE FOR CHICKEN AND TURKEY

1 onion, finely chopped
1 clove of garlic, crushed
2×15ml spoons/2 tablespoons cooking oil
250g/8oz canned tomatoes
1×15ml spoon/1 tablespoon concentrated tomato
purée
1×2.5ml spoon/½ teaspoon fennel seed
1×2.5ml spoon/½ teaspoon dried thyme
1×2.5ml spoon/½ teaspoon dried tarragon
salt, pepper

Gently fry the onion and garlic for about 5 minutes until soft. Add all the remaining ingredients, and bring to the boil. Simmer for 10 minutes. Sieve, or purée in a blender, and use to baste the meat towards the end of the cooking time. Re-heat any remaining baste and serve as a sauce with the cooked meat.

LIGHT CURRY MARINADE FOR CHICKEN

3×15ml spoons/3 tablespoons cooking oil
2×15ml spoons/2 tablespoons lemon juice
1–2×5ml spoons/1–2 teaspoons curry powder
a small clove of garlic, crushed (optional)

Place all the ingredients in a bowl, and mix well together. Dry the chicken or chicken joints and place in the marinade, spooning some of the mixture over the meat. Leave to stand in a cool place for at least 2 hours.

Note This marinade can be used to baste the chicken from the start of the cooking time.

PINEAPPLE MARINADE FOR DUCK

6×15ml spoons/6 tablespoons pineapple juice
2×15ml spoons/2 tablespoons dry cider
3×15ml spoons/3 tablespoons cider vinegar
2×15ml spoons/2 tablespoons soy sauce
1×15ml spoon/1 tablespoon clear honey
1×15ml spoon/1 tablespoon cooking oil

Mix all the ingredients together, and stir until the honey has dissolved. Pre-cook the duck in the oven and leave to cool. Place in the marinade, and spoon the mixture over the top. Leave to stand in a refrigerator for 4–6 hours, turning once or twice.

Barbecued Poultry

CHICKEN TERIYAKI

50ml/2floz light soy sauce
50ml/2floz saki **or** dry sherry
50ml/2floz cooking oil
1×15ml spoon/1 tablespoon soft brown sugar
1 onion, sliced
4 chicken breasts, boned
salt, pepper

Mix the soy sauce, saki or sherry and the cooking oil with the sugar. Stir well to dissolve the sugar. Add the sliced onion and the chicken breasts. Leave to stand in a cool place for at least 2 hours, turning the meat occasionally.

Remove the chicken from the marinade and season all over. Grill over the barbecue for about 5–7 minutes on each side, brushing with a little more marinade from time to time. Heat any remaining marinade, strain, and serve with the chicken.

TARRAGON CHICKEN

4 chicken joints
4×15ml spoons/4 tablespoons cooking oil
2×15ml spoons/2 tablespoons freshly chopped
tarragon **or**
1×15ml spoon/1 tablespoon dried tarragon
salt, freshly ground black pepper
1×15ml spoon/1 tablespoon wine **or** cider vinegar

Place the chicken joints in a large shallow bowl. Mix the remaining ingredients together and pour over the chicken. Leave to stand for 3–4 hours, turning occasionally.

Place on the barbecue to grill, cut side down, and grill for 10 minutes. Turn the joints over and cook on the other side for another 10 minutes. Continue cooking and turning for a further 5–10 minutes, depending on the size of the joints, until the chicken is cooked through. Test by running a skewer or fork into the thickest part of the flesh or towards the joint. The juices should run clear.

MARINATED DRUMSTICKS

8 chicken drumsticks
2×15ml spoons/2 tablespoons concentrated tomato
purée
1 clove of garlic, crushed
juice of $\frac{1}{2}$ lemon
1×15ml spoon/1 tablespoon cider vinegar
1×5ml spoon/1 teaspoon dark brown sugar
$\frac{1}{2}$×2.5ml spoon/$\frac{1}{4}$ teaspoon chilli powder

Wrap the drumsticks in foil and bake at 190°C/375°F/Gas 5 for 30 minutes. Unwrap and place in a shallow bowl. Mix the remaining ingredients together and pour over the chicken. Cool, then stand in a refrigerator for at least 2 hours or until required.

Grill on the barbecue for 15 minutes, turning 3–4 times. Baste with the remaining marinade as required.

CUMIN CHICKEN

1×15ml spoon/1 tablespoon whole cumin seeds
6–8 black peppercorns
4 cardamon pods with the skins removed
2×15ml spoons/2 tablespoons cooking oil
2 onions, finely chopped
2×15ml spoons/2 tablespoons ground cumin
1×15ml spoon/1 tablespoon ground coriander
1×5ml spoon/1 teaspoon turmeric (optional)
150ml/$\frac{1}{4}$ pint natural yoghurt
1×5ml spoon/1 teaspoon lemon juice
4 chicken portions

Fry the cumin seeds, peppercorns and cardamon pods in the cooking oil for 1 minute. Add the onions, and fry until lightly browned. Stir in the spices. Continue cooking for a further minute or two, then remove from the heat and leave to cool.

Stir in the yoghurt and lemon juice, and coat each piece of chicken with the mixture. Place in a bowl, spooning any excess over the top. Cover, and leave in a cool place for at least 2 hours or overnight if possible.

To cook, shake off any excess marinade, brush with a little cooking oil, and grill over the barbecue for 10–15 minutes on each side so that the flesh is scorched on the outside but tender inside.

Note The turmeric, if used, will give a stronger yellow colour to the chicken.

Baby Chicken on a Spit (page 31)

PEPPERED TURKEY STEAKS

600g/1¼lb turkey meat, breast, **or** thigh
juice of 3 lemons
2×15ml spoons/2 tablespoons cider **or** wine vinegar
2×15ml spoons/2 tablespoons cooking oil
1 bay leaf
salt
2×15ml spoons/2 tablespoons mild mustard
1×15ml spoon/1 tablespoon coarsely ground black
pepper

Cut the turkey meat into four steaks or pieces, and place in a bowl. Mix the lemon juice, vinegar and oil and pour it over the top of the meat. Add the bay leaf and leave to stand in a cool place for at least 2 hours.

Drain the meat, and season with salt. Mix the mustard and black pepper, and spread thinly over the meat. Grill over the barbecue for 10–15 minutes on each side.

TURKEY BUTTERFLIES WITH REDCURRANT GLAZE

150ml/¼pint red wine
1 small onion, sliced
1 bouquet garni
2–3 turkey legs
2×15ml spoons/2 tablespoons cooking oil
salt, pepper
3×15ml spoons/3 tablespoons redcurrant jelly

Pour the wine into a large bowl. Add the onion and bouquet garni. Make a cut along the length of each leg and cut out the bone. Flatten the flesh and place in the bowl with the wine. Leave to stand in a cool place for at least 2 hours.

Drain the meat, retaining the marinade. Brush with oil, then season to taste. Grill over the barbecue for about 10–15 minutes on each side, brushing with a little more oil as required.

Meanwhile, melt the redcurrant jelly in a saucepan. About 5 minutes before the end of the cooking time, brush first one side of each turkey leg and then the other with hot redcurrant jelly, and return to the grill. Add any remaining jelly to the marinade and bring to the boil. Reduce by a third, sieve, and serve with the turkey. Cut the meat into chunks or slices to serve.

SPATCHCOCK CHICKEN WITH PRUNE SAUCE

2 spring chickens
50g/2oz butter, melted
salt, pepper

SAUCE
100g/4oz dried prunes, soaked overnight
150ml/¼pint chicken stock
1×15ml spoon/1 tablespoon cider **or** wine vinegar

Make the sauce first. Put the prunes into a saucepan, add the stock, vinegar and salt and pepper, and bring to the boil. Simmer for 30 minutes, then sieve. Return to the pan, and simmer until fairly thick.

Split the chickens in half, cutting through the backbone. Flatten out the bird, removing the breastbone if necessary. Break the joints to make flattening easier. Brush all over with melted butter, and season well. Place bone side down over the barbecue and cook for 10 minutes. Turn over and cook the second side for 10 minutes. Brush with more butter and turn twice again until the chickens are cooked.

Serve with the prune sauce.

Note If liked, the outside of the chicken can be basted with the sauce, then finished off and served with the remaining sauce in a sauce-boat.

BABY CHICKEN ON A SPIT

100g/4oz clear honey
4 lumps crystallized stem ginger in honey **or** syrup,
finely chopped
150ml/¼ pint orange juice
2×15ml spoons/2 tablespoons cider **or** wine vinegar
4 very small poussins **or** 2 small chickens
cooking oil
salt, pepper
a knob of butter

Mix the honey, ginger, orange juice and vinegar, and stir until the honey has dissolved. Arrange the chickens in a deep dish and pour the marinade over the top. Leave to stand in a cool place for at least 2 hours, turning the chickens every 15–20 minutes. Drain well, retaining the marinade.

Skewer the chickens with the spit, making sure that the birds are well balanced and that the wings and legs are securely anchored down. Brush all over with cooking oil, and season well, then spit-roast for about 1 hour for the poussins and 1½–2 hours for the small chickens. Brush with more oil from time to time. Test the flesh with a skewer; if the juices run clear the birds are cooked. Towards the end of the cooking time, heat the marinade with a knob of butter, and boil for 5–8 minutes to give a sweet sauce.

ORANGE BARBECUED DUCK

1 duck
1 onion, sliced
1 bay leaf
juice and grated rind of 2 oranges
2×15ml spoons/2 tablespoons cider vinegar
2×15ml spoons/2 tablespoons dark brown sugar
1×15ml spoon/1 tablespoon cooking oil
1×2.5ml spoon/½ teaspoon ground ginger
1×2.5ml spoon/½ teaspoon ground coriander
a pinch of allspice

Prick the duck all over with a fork, and roast, breast down, at 200°C/400°F/Gas 6, for 1 hour. Joint the duck, and leave to cool. Place in a bowl with the sliced onion and bay leaf. Mix all the remaining ingredients and pour them over the top. Leave to stand for at least 2 hours in a cool place, turning from time to time.

Drain the joints and retain the marinade. Place the joints on the grill, bone side down, and cook for 10 minutes. Turn over, and cook for a further 5 minutes, basting with the marinade towards the end of the cooking time.

STEAKS AND THINGS

Although almost any kind of meat can be cooked on a barbecue, all but the most expensive cuts will need to be marinated before cooking. As barbecue cooking is a fast method of cooking, tough meat needs to be tenderized first.

The best cuts of beef to grill on the barbecue are fillet, sirloin and rump steaks which probably do not need to be marinated, and flank, skirt and topside which do need to be marinated. Do not have the steaks cut too thinly or they will quickly overcook. Larger joints like rolled sirloin or topside are excellent for spit-roasting. Topside is so lean that it may need to be marinated first.

Virtually all lamb cuts can be barbecued, the easiest ones being single and double cutlets and loin and chump chops. Strictly speaking, marinating is not necessary for these cuts but it can help to highlight the flavour. Frozen lamb can be thawed in the marinade.

Breast of lamb and scrag end or middle neck chops tend to be rather fatty and so they should be cooked first and then marinated for flavour before grilling on the barbecue. Legs and shoulders are less obvious cuts to choose but they can be boned and laid flat on the grill or rolled and cooked on the spit.

Pork chops are also easy to barbecue but the flesh tends to dry up quickly, and therefore often needs to be marinated to increase the juiciness of the meat. It is important to cook all pork until well done. Chops are the best cut to use for grilling, but you could also try pork steaks. Sausages are, of course, excellent for barbecuing, being both cheap and extremely easy to cook. Gammon can also be cooked on the barbecue, but must be well basted to keep from drying out.

Like pork, veal usually needs to be marinated to retain flavour and juiciness. Baste well while cooking.

Basic Preparation and Cooking

Whatever meat you choose, trim off all the excess fat before cooking. This helps to keep fat flares to a minimum. Score any remaining fat on chops and steaks to prevent it curling up.

The meat should be at room temperature for cooking. Season with pepper, herbs, spices and mustard but leave the salt until after the meat is cooked. Salt tends to draw the juices and this can spoil the meat and cause flares.

To grill, brush the pieces of meat with a very little oil. However, this is not necessary if the meat has been marinated in a marinade containing cooking oil. Place on the grill, making sure that there is at least a 7.5cm/3 inch gap between the charcoal and the grill. If you think there may be a tendency for fat to fall on the coals, from sausages for example, set the grill a little higher.

As soon as the first side is sealed, turn the meat over and seal the second side. Continue to turn frequently during cooking as this helps to keep the juices inside the meat. If using a basting sauce, paint on with a brush during the second half of the cooking time. Avoid brushing the baste on too thickly or it may fall off again.

To cook sausages, place them across the bars of the grill so that they do not fall through. Grill for about 10 minutes, bearing in mind that they will shrink. Chipolatas take a shorter time to cook than do thicker sausages. If you think they will be very fatty, cook for 10 minutes in advance to release the fat, and then finish off on the barbecue.

Spit-roasting meat is even easier than spit-roasting poultry. Have the meat boned and rolled, and make sure that the skewer passes straight through the centre so that the meat is evenly balanced and will not cause a strain on the motor. Beef and lamb may be served pink but, as stated earlier, pork should be well done, and a meat thermometer is the safest way of ensuring that large pieces of meat are thoroughly cooked. A drip tray will also be necessary; this can be made as described on page 17.

CHART OF COOKING TIMES

Meat and cuts	grill		spit-roast
Beef	*medium rare*	*medium*	
steaks	6–10 minutes depending on size	9–15 minutes depending on size	–
sirloin, boned and rolled	–	–	20 minutes per 500g/1 lb
topside, boned and rolled	–	–	25 minutes per 500g/1 lb
Lamb			
loin and chump chops	10–15 minutes	15–20 minutes	–
cutlets	8–12 minutes	10–15 minutes	–
shoulder, boned and rolled	–	–	25 minutes per 500g/1 lb
leg	–	–	25 minutes per 500g/1 lb
Pork			
chops	–	20–25 minutes	–
spare ribs (pre-cooked)	–	8–10 minutes	–
steaks	–	15–20 minutes	–
sausages	–	8–15 minutes depending on size	–
gammon steak	–	10–12 minutes	–
Veal			
chops	–	8–10 minutes depending on thickness	–

Marinades and Bastes

Most meats benefit from marinating. As stated earlier, the longer the meat is left in the marinade the better flavour it will have and the more tender it will be; lamb and beef can safely be kept in a marinade for up to 3 days. Always keep marinating meat in a cool place or in a refrigerator, and bring it up to room temperature for an hour or so before cooking.

RED WINE MARINADE FOR BEEF

100ml/4 fl oz red wine
100ml/4 fl oz cooking oil
1 small onion, cut into rings
1 clove of garlic, crushed
1 bay leaf
a pinch of mustard
freshly ground black pepper

Mix all the ingredients together and pour over the meat. Leave to stand in a cool place for 24 hours, and turn from time to time.

ORANGE TARRAGON MARINADE FOR LAMB

juice and grated rind of 1 large orange
2 × 15ml spoons / 2 tablespoons natural yoghurt
1 × 5ml spoon / 1 teaspoon dried tarragon leaves
freshly ground black pepper

Mix all the ingredients together and pour over the meat. Leave to stand for at least 2 hours in a cool place, and turn from time to time.

CURRY MARINADE FOR ANY MEAT

1 chicken stock cube
100ml/4 fl oz boiling water
150ml/$\frac{1}{4}$ pint tomato ketchup
1 × 15ml spoon / 1 tablespoon lemon juice
1 × 15ml spoon / 1 tablespoon curry powder
freshly ground black pepper

Dissolve the stock cube in the boiling water and mix in the remaining ingredients. Leave to cool. Pour over the meat and leave to stand for at least 2 hours in a cool place. Turn the meat from time to time.

Beer Marinade for Beef or Sausages

150ml/¼ pint beer **or** brown ale
1×15ml spoon/1 tablespoon dark brown sugar
1 onion, cut into rings
rind and juice of ½ lemon
4×15ml spoons/4 tablespoons cooking oil
1 clove
freshly ground black pepper

Gently heat the beer and sugar, stirring until the sugar has dissolved. Add the remaining ingredients and leave to cool. Pour over the meat and leave to stand in a cool place overnight. Turn the meat occasionally.

Herb Marinade for Lamb or Pork

150ml/¼ pint dry cider
2×15ml spoons/2 tablespoons cooking oil
2×15ml spoons/2 tablespoons cider vinegar
1 small onion, very finely chopped
4×15ml spoons/4 tablespoons freshly chopped parsley
1×15ml spoon/1 tablespoon freshly chopped mint
1×2.5ml spoon/½ teaspoon dried rosemary
freshly ground black pepper

Mix all the ingredients together and pour over the meat. Marinate overnight in a refrigerator.

Note Enough for 1kg/2 lb meat

Apple Basting Sauce for Pork or Gammon

1 onion, finely chopped
1 clove of garlic, crushed
2×15ml spoons/2 tablespoons cooking oil
1 cooking apple, grated
2×15ml spoons/2 tablespoons clear honey
150ml/¼ pint apple juice
2×15ml spoons/2 tablespoons cider vinegar
1×15ml spoon/1 tablespoon Worcestershire sauce
1×5ml spoon/1 teaspoon made mustard
freshly ground black pepper
a pinch of dried thyme

Gently fry the onion and garlic in cooking oil for about 5 minutes until tender. Add the cooking apple, and cook for a further 2–3 minutes. Stir in the honey and the remaining ingredients. Leave to cool and use to marinate the meat for an hour or so, or use as a baste during cooking, heating up any remaining sauce to serve with the meat.

Orange Basting Sauce for Lamb, Pork or Ham

4×15ml spoons/4 tablespoons orange marmalade
juice of 1 lemon
1×15ml spoon/1 tablespoon brown sugar
juice and grated rind of 1 orange
2×15ml spoons/2 tablespoons raisins

Put all the ingredients into a pan and bring to the boil, stirring all the time. Simmer for 5 minutes, and use hot. Serve any remaining sauce with the meat.

BARBECUE BASTE FOR LAMB

300ml/½ pint olive oil
4×15ml spoons/4 tablespoons lemon juice
1 small onion, finely chopped
2×15ml spoons/2 tablespoons freshly chopped parsley
freshly ground black pepper
2–3 drops Tabasco sauce

Mix all the ingredients together and leave the mixture to stand for an hour before using.

Note Use also as a marinade, leaving the meat in the mixture for an hour or so.

Barbecued Beef, Lamb and Pork

BEEF TERIYAKI

750g/1½ lb flank **or** skirt beef
75ml/3 fl oz soy sauce
75ml/3 fl oz saki **or** dry sherry
50ml/2 fl oz cooking oil
1 small onion, sliced
2.5cm/1 inch fresh root ginger, peeled and chopped
salt, black pepper

Beat the meat between two sheets of greaseproof paper and cut into steaks. Place in a large shallow dish. Mix all the remaining ingredients and pour over the meat. Leave to stand in a cool place overnight.

Drain the meat and grill over the barbecue for 3–4 minutes for rare steaks, longer for medium or well-done steaks.

STEAK AU POIVRE

4×15ml spoons/4 tablespoons crushed **or** coarsely ground black peppercorns
1×5ml spoon/1 teaspoon mild French mustard
1–2×5ml spoons/1–2 teaspoons red **or** white wine
4 small rump **or** sirloin steaks
cooking oil

Mix the peppercorns, mustard and wine to make a thick paste. Spread a little on each side of each steak, and leave in a cool place for 2 hours.

Brush the steaks with a very little oil, and grill over the barbecue for 3–6 minutes on each side, depending on how well cooked you like them.

LEMON AND GINGER LAMB STRIPS

2 large breasts of lamb
rind and juice of 2 lemons
1.25cm/½ inch fresh root ginger, peeled and finely chopped
2×15ml spoons/2 tablespoons marmalade
cooking oil
salt, pepper

Cut the meat into strips along the bones. Place on a baking tray and roast at 190°C/375°F/Gas 5 for 40 minutes. Drain and place in a shallow dish. Mix the remaining ingredients and pour over the meat. Leave to cool and then stand in a refrigerator for 3–4 hours, turning the pieces of meat from time to time.

Drain the meat before cooking, and brush with oil. Season, and grill over the barbecue for about 6–8 minutes on each side.

Lemon and Ginger Lamb Strips and *Lamburgers (page 46) with Apple and Corn Relish (page 43) and Sauerkraut Relish (page 43)*

INDIAN LAMB CHOPS

1 large onion, chopped
1×15ml spoon/1 tablespoon cooking oil
2–3×15ml spoons/2–3 tablespoons curry powder
1×15ml spoon/1 tablespoon whole cumin seeds
2×5ml spoons/2 teaspoons ground coriander
3 cardamon pods
150ml/¼pint water
1×5ml spoon/1 teaspoon concentrated tomato purée
juice of ½ lemon
8 best end of neck lamb cutlets

Fry the onion in oil for 2–3 minutes. Stir in the curry powder and spices, and cook for a minute, stirring all the time. Add the water, tomato purée and lemon juice. Mix well and bring to the boil. Cover, and simmer for 15 minutes, then cool.

Place the lamb cutlets in a shallow bowl. Pour the curry sauce mixture over the top, and marinate for 2–3 hours, turning the cutlets from time to time.

Grill the chops over the barbecue, allowing about 5 minutes each side. Baste with any remaining sauce during cooking.

CHOPS IN A PARCEL

2 onions, finely chopped
1×15ml spoon/1 tablespoon cooking oil
2 large tomatoes, peeled and chopped
1×15ml spoon/1 tablespoon mango chutney
salt, pepper
4 lamb loin chips

Fry the onions in the oil until they soften. Add the tomatoes, chutney and seasoning. Stir and remove from the heat. Place each chop on a piece of aluminium foil, season well and top with the onion and tomato mixture. Wrap up into four foil parcels, making sure that the meat and topping are completely sealed in. Cook on the barbecue for 40–50 minutes.

BUTTERFLY LAMB

1 leg of lamb, boned
150ml/¼ pint dry white wine
4×15ml spoons/4 tablespoons lemon juice
2×15ml spoons/2 tablespoons Worcestershire sauce
2×15ml spoons/2 tablespoons cooking oil
1–2 cloves garlic, crushed
1×5ml spoon/1 teaspoon dried basil
1×5ml spoon/1 teaspoon dried rosemary
1×5ml spoon/1 teaspoon dried marjoram
salt, pepper

Open the leg out flat and place in a shallow dish. Mix all the remaining ingredients together and pour over the meat. Cover and leave to stand in a refrigerator for at least 24 hours.

Drain the meat, and place over the barbecue, making sure that the meat is not too near the coals. Sprinkle the coals with more herbs, and grill for 25 minutes on each side. Leave the meat to rest for 5–10 minutes before carving and serving.

SWEET AND SOUR PORK

4 pork steaks **or** chops
juice of 1 lemon
2×15ml spoons/2 tablespoons vinegar
75ml/3 fl oz apple **or** orange juice
1 bay leaf
black pepper
cooking oil

Place the pork in a shallow dish. Mix the lemon juice and vinegar with the fruit juice, and pour this liquid over the pork. Add a bay leaf and some black pepper. Leave to stand in a cool place for 2 hours or more.

Drain the meat, brush with a little oil, and grill over the barbecue for about 20–25 minutes, turning from time to time.

BARBECUED SPARE RIBS

12 ripe apricots **or** 2 medium cooking apples
3 × 15ml spoons / 3 tablespoons water
1.5kg/3lb spare ribs, cut into strips between the bones
25ml/1floz apricot brandy **or** Calvados
50ml/2floz cider vinegar
2 × 15ml spoons / 2 tablespoons soy sauce
175g/6oz brown sugar
1 clove of garlic, crushed
$\frac{1}{2}$ × 2.5ml spoon / $\frac{1}{4}$ teaspoon ground ginger
black pepper

Stone the apricots or peel, core and slice the apple thinly. Put into a pan with the water, and simmer until soft. Sieve, or purée in a blender. Put to one side.

Place the spare ribs in a pan, and cover with water. Bring to the boil, cover and simmer for 40 minutes. Drain well and place in a shallow dish. Mix together all the remaining ingredients, including the purée, and pour over the meat. Cool, and then stand in a refrigerator overnight. Turn the ribs from time to time.

Drain well and place on the grill. Cook for about 6–8 minutes on each side, basting with any remaining marinade towards the end of the cooking time.

GRILLED GAMMON

4 gammon steaks
cooking oil
1 × 2.5ml spoon / $\frac{1}{2}$ teaspoon ground coriander
a pinch of ground cardamon
salt, pepper

Trim the steaks and make 0.5cm/$\frac{1}{4}$ inch cuts at 2.5cm/1 inch intervals along the fatty edge. Brush with cooking oil, and sprinkle with spices and seasoning. Grill on the barbecue for 5–6 minutes each side, depending on the thickness of the steaks. Brush with oil during cooking to prevent the steaks drying out too much.

BARBECUED BACON STEAKS

5 × 15ml spoons / 5 tablespoons tomato ketchup
2 × 15ml spoons / 2 tablespoons cider vinegar
2 × 5ml spoons / 2 teaspoons sugar
3–4 drops Tabasco sauce
4 round bacon steaks
freshly ground black pepper

Mix the tomato ketchup, vinegar, sugar and Tabasco sauce to a smooth purée. Spread the mixture over both sides of each bacon steak, and leave to stand for at least 1 hour.

Season each steak with black pepper, and grill over the barbecue for about 6–8 minutes on each side until the baste has bubbled and thickened on the steaks.

VEAL CHOPS WITH BASIL

4 veal chops
3–4 sprigs fresh basil
juice of 1 lemon
4 × 15ml spoons / 4 tablespoons cooking oil
freshly ground black pepper

Make some small slits in the chops and insert a few leaves of fresh basil. Place the chops in a shallow dish, and cover with lemon juice, oil and pepper. Leave to stand in a cool place for an hour or so.

Drain, retaining the marinade, and sprinkle with the remaining basil. Place the chops on the barbecue and grill for about 8–10 minutes on each side, depending on the thickness of the chops. Baste from time to time by brushing with a little of the marinade.

Note Do not overcook the chops, as veal dries up very quickly.

MARINATED HOTDOGS

8 hotdog sausages
4×15ml spoons/4 tablespoons red wine
1×5ml spoon/1 teaspoon lemon juice
1×15ml spoon/1 tablespoon cooking oil
1×2.5ml spoon/½ teaspoon dried rosemary
1×5ml spoon/1 teaspoon brown sugar
8 rashers streaky bacon, without rinds

Prick the sausages all over with a sharp fork and arrange in a shallow dish. Mix all the remaining ingredients except the bacon, and stir until the sugar has dissolved. Pour over the sausages, and leave to stand in a cool place for at least 2 hours.

Drain the sausages well and wrap a piece of streaky bacon round each one, covering as much of the sausages as possible. Secure at each end with half a cocktail stick. Grill over the coolest part of the barbecue for about 6–8 minutes, turning from time to time, until the bacon is crisp and brown.

APPLE-GLAZED SAUSAGES

12 sausages (750g/1½ lb)
150ml/¼ pint apple sauce
2×15ml spoons/2 tablespoons cider vinegar
1×15ml spoon/1 tablespoon dark brown sugar
½×2.5ml spoon/¼ teaspoon powdered cloves

Place the sausages in a baking tin and bake at 190°C/375°F/Gas 5 for 30 minutes. Remove from the oven, prick all over with a fork and place in a bowl. Mix the remaining ingredients together and pour over the sausages. When they are cold, chill in a refrigerator for 2 hours or more until required. Grill over the barbecue for about 10 minutes, turning from time to time.

BARBECUE PANCAKES

12 sausages (500g/1 lb)
4×15ml spoons/4 tablespoons any relish

PANCAKES
100g/4oz plain flour
½×2.5ml spoon/¼ teaspoon salt
1 egg
300ml/½ pint milk

Make the pancakes first, ahead of time. Mix together the flour, salt and egg. Stir in half the milk, and beat until smooth. Stir in the remaining milk. Pour enough batter into a lightly greased pan to make one pancake, and continue until all the batter has been used. Leave to cool.

Layer the pancakes between sheets of lightly greased foil, and warm over the coolest part of the barbecue. Cook the sausages over the barbecue until well browned all over. Spread each pancake with your chosen relish, and place one sausage in each. Roll up and serve at once.

Chops in a Parcel (page 38) and Barbecued Spare Ribs (page 39)

Hamburger Bonanza

Hamburgers are one of the quickest and easiest items to cook over the barbecue. Choose a good quality mince or buy chuck steak or flank and have this minced for you by the butcher. Too fatty a mixture will drip fat on to the coals and the resultant flare up could easily burn the burgers.

The idea of pressing freshly minced meat into cakes and cooking them has been popular for quite some time. The meat need not just be beef. Lamb makes excellent burgers and a beef and pork mixture is also very good. Some butchers already sell minced lamb or minced pork but even if they do not have it already prepared, they will certainly mince your choice of cut on request. So vary your mixtures and add a little chopped onion, herbs or garlic to suit your taste.

Basic Cooking Method

Do not press the meat too closely together or the resultant burger will be rather dry. If you are worried that the burgers will fall apart, use a special wire mesh grill to hold them. Set the grill rack a little higher than for steaks, and grill for about 5–10 minutes each side depending on size and on how well-done you like your burgers to be. Hamburgers with pork or sausage-meat should be cooked for the longer times.

Part of the popularity of hamburgers rests with the bun, sauces and relishes with which they are served. Buy real sesame buns and set out a selection of sauces and relishes for guests to choose from. Buy proprietary brands and mixes for speed and make a few of your own for variety.

Gooseberry Chutney

1kg/2 lb gooseberries, topped and tailed
600ml/1 pint malt vinegar
250g/8 oz soft brown sugar
250g/8 oz onions
375g/12 oz raisins
50g/2 oz mustard seed
25g/1 oz ground allspice
25g/1 oz salt

Put the gooseberries into a saucepan with half the vinegar. Bring to the boil, then simmer for 15–20 minutes until tender. Mix the sugar and the rest of the vinegar and pour into another pan. Bring to the boil and simmer for 15 minutes. Add the onions, raisins, mustard seed, allspice and salt, then simmer for a further 15 minutes. Add the gooseberries and their liquor. Continue to simmer for about 1 hour until the mixture is thick and brown. Spoon into hot jars, cover and seal.

Note Makes 1.25kg/2½ lb (approx)

Minty Apple Relish

1 apple, peeled, cored and grated
juice of 1 lemon
150g/5 oz natural yoghurt
4 × 15ml spoons / 4 tablespoons sweet mint jelly
1 × 5ml spoon / 1 teaspoon vinegar
salt, pepper

Mix the apple and lemon juice to prevent discoloration. Stir in the yoghurt, mint jelly and vinegar, and season to taste.

SAUERKRAUT RELISH

375g/12 oz sauerkraut
100g/4 oz sugar
1×2.5ml spoon/½ teaspoon celery salt
½ green pepper, de-seeded and very finely chopped
½ red pepper, de-seeded and very finely chopped

Mix all the ingredients together and place in a covered container. Leave to marinate for 24 hours.

APPLE AND CORN RELISH

250g/8 oz onions, chopped
500g/1 lb cooking apples, peeled, cored and sliced
250g/8 oz sweetcorn kernels
2×15ml spoons/2 tablespoons concentrated tomato
purée
75g/3 oz sugar
150ml/¼ pint vinegar
1×2.5ml spoon/½ teaspoon allspice
1×2.5ml spoon/½ teaspoon mixed herbs
salt, pepper

Put all the ingredients into a large saucepan. Bring gradually to the boil, stirring to dissolve the sugar. Cover the pan and simmer for 2–2½ hours until the mixture is thick and pulpy. Spoon into hot jars, cover and seal. Leave for at least a week before using. Once open, store in a refrigerator.

Note Makes 1kg/2 lb (approx)

FRUIT SAUCE

500g/1 lb tomatoes, chopped
375g/12 oz cooking apples, cored and chopped
250g/8 oz onions, sliced
100g/4 oz dates, stoned and chopped
250g/8 oz raisins
300ml/½ pint vinegar
1×5ml spoon/1 teaspoon salt
1×2.5ml spoon/½ teaspoon ground ginger
½×2.5ml spoon/¼ teaspoon ground cloves
½×2.5ml spoon/¼ teaspoon mixed spices
a pinch of Cayenne pepper
250g/8 oz soft brown sugar

Put all the ingredients, except the sugar, into a pan, and bring to the boil. Simmer for 1 hour and sieve, or purée in a blender. Add the sugar, and return to the pan. Stir over low heat until all the sugar has dissolved. Bring to the boil and simmer for 45 minutes until thick. Spoon into hot jars, cover and seal.

Note If you do not use this quantity of sauce at one barbecue, it will keep in a refrigerator for 2–3 weeks.

BLUE CHEESE HAMBURGER TOPPING

75g/3 oz blue cheese, crumbled
50g/2 oz butter, softened
1 clove of garlic, crushed (optional)
25g/1 oz walnuts, chopped
1×15ml spoon/1 tablespoon freshly chopped chives

Mix the cheese, butter and garlic to a smooth paste. Stir in the walnuts and chives. Shape into a rectangular block about 5cm/2 inches across, then chill. Cut into slices and use to top beef or lamb burgers.

HORSERADISH HAMBURGER TOPPING

150ml/¼ pint mayonnaise
2×15ml spoons/2 tablespoons creamed horseradish
2×5ml spoons/2 teaspoons tomato ketchup
salt, pepper

Mix all the ingredients together, and use to top beef or beef and pork burgers.

Barbecued Hamburgers

SWEDISH HAMBURGERS

1 small onion
15g/½ oz butter
500g/1 lb minced beef
2 egg yolks
1×15ml spoon/1 tablespoon vinegar
4×15ml spoons/4 tablespoons double cream
2×15ml spoons/2 tablespoons capers, finely chopped
3 small whole pickled beets, finely chopped
salt, pepper

Fry the onion in butter until soft. Put into a bowl with the meat, egg yolks, vinegar and cream, and mix to a smooth paste. Stir in the capers and beetroot, and season to taste. Shape into four burgers and grill over the barbecue for 3–4 minutes each side. If you do not like your hamburgers to be pink inside, cook for a little longer but remember that the beetroot tends to make the meat look pink even when it is fully cooked.

CLAIRE'S BRUNCH BURGERS

600g/1¼ lb minced steak
1 medium onion, finely chopped
1 large clove of garlic, finely chopped
1×15ml spoon/1 tablespoon Worcestershire sauce
2×5ml spoons/2 teaspoons tomato ketchup
salt, freshly ground black pepper
6–7 drops Tabasco sauce
1½×5ml spoons/1½ teaspoons mixed herbs

Place all the ingredients in a large bowl, and mix well together. Shape into four large balls. Flatten slightly and leave to stand for 1 hour before placing on the barbecue. Grill for 2½–3 minutes on each side for rare burgers and 5–6 minutes for well-done burgers.

SPICED BEEF AND RICE BURGERS

50g/2 oz long grain rice
salt
100ml/4 fl oz water
500g/1 lb minced beef
2×5ml spoons/2 teaspoons Worcestershire sauce
2×5ml spoons/2 teaspoons ground cumin
½×2.5ml spoon/¼ teaspoon ground chilli
salt, pepper

Cook the rice in boiling salted water, stir, then cover. Cook for about 10–12 minutes until all the water has been absorbed. Mix with the beef and other ingredients. Shape into four burgers and cook on both sides for about 3–4 minutes each side.

Preparing Stuffed Hamburgers (2) (page 46)

TEXAN HAMBURGERS

100g/4oz concentrated tomato purée
3×15ml spoons/3 tablespoons tomato ketchup
1×15ml spoon/1 tablespoon Worcestershire sauce
2×15ml spoons/2 tablespoons vinegar
juice of 1 lemon
1×15ml spoon/1 tablespoon brown sugar
4 shallots **or** 8 spring onions, finely chopped
1×2.5ml spoon/½ teaspoon garlic salt
2–3 drops Tabasco sauce
600g/1¼lb minced beef

Put all the ingredients, except the beef, into a saucepan, and bring to the boil, stirring all the time. Simmer for 10 minutes, stirring occasionally. Remove from the heat and leave to cool. Add 5–6×15ml spoons/5–6 tablespoons of the sauce to the beef, and mix thoroughly. Shape into four burgers and grill over the barbecue for 4–5 minutes each side, basting with the remaining sauce towards the end of the cooking time. Use any leftover sauce to spread on burger buns or to fill baked potatoes.

STUFFED HAMBURGERS (1)

salt, pepper
500g/1lb minced steak
4 spring onions, finely chopped
25g/1oz Cheddar cheese, grated

Season the minced steak and divide into four portions. Mix the onion and cheese and form into four small balls. Shape each portion of meat round one of the balls so that the filling is completely enclosed. Flatten slightly to a hamburger shape. Grill over the barbecue for 3–4 minutes on each side.

STUFFED HAMBURGERS (2)

4×5ml spoons/4 teaspoons minty apple relish (p42)
2 fresh ripe apricots, halved and stoned
salt, pepper
600g/1¼lb minced beef

Place 1×5ml spoon/1 teaspoon of relish in the cavity of each apricot half. Season the beef and divide into four equal parts. Take a half of one of the portions and flatten out in your hand. Place the stuffed apricot in the centre and cover with the second half. Carefully shape into a hamburger, making sure that the apricot is completely sealed in. Repeat this process with the remaining three hamburgers. Grill over the barbecue for 4–5 minutes on each side or a little longer if you like your hamburgers well done.

LAMBURGERS

1 small onion, finely chopped
1 stick of celery, finely chopped
2×15ml spoons/2 tablespoons cooking oil
600g/1¼lb minced lamb
50g/2oz fresh breadcrumbs
2×5ml spoons/2 teaspoons tomato ketchup
1×5ml spoon/1 teaspoon Worcestershire sauce
1×2.5ml spoon/½ teaspoon mixed herbs
salt, pepper

Gently fry the onion and celery in the cooking oil for about 5 minutes until tender. Do not allow to brown. Remove from the heat and mix with all the remaining ingredients. Shape into four burgers and grill over the barbecue for about 6–7 minutes on each side.

MIDDLE EASTERN LAMB BURGERS

600g/1¼ lb lean boned lamb
6×15ml spoons/6 tablespoons freshly chopped parsley
or 1½×15ml spoons/1½ tablespoons dried parsley
2×15ml spoons/2 tablespoons freshly chopped mint **or**
1×5ml spoon/1 teaspoon dried mint
1×5ml spoon/1 teaspoon ground coriander
a pinch of cinnamon
salt, pepper

Mince the lamb or chop finely in a food processor. Add all the remaining ingredients and mix well with a fork. Shape into eight small burgers and chill in a refrigerator. Cook on both sides for about 5–6 minutes on each side.

SHAMI KEBABS

500g/1 lb beef **or** lamb, cut into chunks
2 onions, finely chopped
50g/2 oz split lentils
600ml/1 pint stock
2.5cm/1 inch piece fresh root ginger, finely chopped
2×5ml spoons/2 teaspoons ground cumin
2×5ml spoons/2 teaspoons ground coriander
1×5ml spoon/1 teaspoon poppyseeds
salt, pepper
1 egg, beaten
cooking oil

Place all the ingredients, except the egg, into a pan, and bring to the boil. Reduce the heat, cover, and cook for 30 minutes. Remove the lid and turn up the heat to evaporate any remaining liquid. Leave to cool a little and then mince or chop in a food processor. Mix with the egg, and leave to cool.

Shape the mixture into eight small cakes. Brush with oil and grill over the barbecue for 3–4 minutes on each side. If the kebabs show signs of falling apart, wrap loosely in foil, and brown at the end of the cooking time.

FRENCH PORKBURGERS

500g/1 lb spare rib of pork, boned and minced
75g/3 oz stale breadcrumbs
1×5ml spoon/1 teaspoon salt
½×2.5ml spoon/¼ teaspoon black pepper
½×2.5ml spoon/¼ teaspoon paprika
½×2.5ml spoon/¼ teaspoon cinnamon
½×2.5ml spoon/¼ teaspoon allspice
a pinch of nutmeg
2–3 shallots, minced **or** grated
2×15ml spoons/2 tablespoons freshly chopped parsley
1 size 3 egg, beaten
flour

Mix the minced pork with the breadcrumbs, then add the seasoning and spices. Turn the mixture on to a board and knead well. Spread the mixture out and scatter with the shallots and parsley. Knead again to mix thoroughly. Bind with beaten egg and shape into four burgers. Coat very lightly with flour, and grill over the barbecue, placing the grill a little farther away from the coals than usual. Grill for at least 8–10 minutes on each side.

GOOSEBERRY PORKBURGERS

250g/8oz lean pork, minced
250g/8oz sausage-meat
100g/4oz fresh breadcrumbs
3×15ml spoons/3 tablespoons gooseberry chutney
(p42)
salt, pepper

Mix the pork and sausage-meat with half the breadcrumbs and all the gooseberry chutney. Season to taste and beat well with a fork. Shape into four large or eight small cakes. Coat lightly with the remaining breadcrumbs, pushing them well into the meat. Chill for 2 hours and then grill over the barbecue for 5–8 minutes on each side, depending on size.

BACON AND SAUSAGE BURGERS

500g/1lb sausage-meat
100g/4oz lean bacon, finely chopped
1 small onion, grated
1×5ml spoon/1 teaspoon dried mixed herbs
1×5ml spoon/1 teaspoon tomato ketchup **or** made
mustard
salt, pepper
1 size 6 egg, beaten
cooking oil

Mix the sausage-meat, bacon and onion with the herbs, ketchup or mustard and the seasoning. Add sufficient egg to make a smooth but not too sloppy paste. Shape into small burgers, brush with oil, and grill over the barbecue for 5–6 minutes. Brush with oil again and turn over to grill the other side.

SMOKY FISH BURGERS

175g/6oz smoked cod fillet, skinned
50ml/2floz milk
1 hard-boiled egg
175g/6oz cooked potatoes, peeled and mashed
salt, black pepper
1–2×15ml spoons/1–2 tablespoons dry breadcrumbs
cooking oil

Poach the fish in the milk for about 6–8 minutes until tender. Drain well and mince with the egg, or mash with a fork. Mix with the potatoes, and season to taste. Leave to cool.

Shape the mixture into four small cakes, and coat very lightly with dry breadcrumbs, pushing them well into the burger mixture. Brush with cooking oil, and grill over the barbecue for 3–4 minutes on each side.

FISHY FEASTS

Fish and shell fish can be cooked over the barbecue with just the same sort of delicious results as meat and poultry. However, they are very much more delicate and need to be handled with care or they will break up. Both also need to be cooked as quickly as possible or they will go very dry and hard.

Small whole fish like mackerel, trout, herring and plaice, and thick steaks of salmon, cod, hake and halibut can be grilled directly over the coals. A special hinged fish grill with a fine wire mesh to hold the fish in place is extremely useful. It helps to stop the fish breaking up when it is turned and omits the need for keeping a permanent watch over the heat with a fish slice.

Basic Preparation and Cooking

Always use really fresh fish, if possible buying it on the same day as the barbecue party. If you have to buy it the day before, wash well and sprinkle with a little lemon juice, or stand in a marinade overnight. Make sure that frozen fish is fully thawed before using.

Rub the general grill or the fish grill with a little fat before placing the fish on it and do not allow the grill to heat up first, otherwise fish skins and flesh will immediately stick to it. Oil the fish also, basting with a little more fat as the fish cooks, unless it is first being marinated.

Large whole fish such as salmon trout or sea-bass can be cooked on the spit. Salmon is a fairly oily fish and does not need to be basted during cooking. It does, nevertheless, benefit from brushing with a mixture of lemon juice and melted butter towards the end of the cooking time.

Both whole fish and steaks can be cooked with foil. For small fish and steaks, oil the foil well and encase completely with foil, adding any flavourings before the parcel is sealed. Twist the ends of the parcel to prevent steam from escaping, and place in the embers or on the grill. Large fish can be cooked on open pieces of well oiled foil on the grill. Baste the fish during cooking with the marinade and the juices that collect at the base of the fish.

Larger fish will take longer to cook than small ones or steaks, so spread the coals out to lower the temperature and prevent the outside burning before the inside is cooked.

To test if the fish is cooked, try with a fork near to the bones. If the flesh comes away easily, the fish is cooked. For foil parcels, pierce the foil and fish with a skewer. If the fish feels soft and the skewer comes out clean, the fish will be cooked.

CHART OF COOKING TIMES			
Fish	**open grill**	**foil grill**	**spit-roast**
white fish steaks cod, halibut, etc	5–10 minutes depending on size	10–15 minutes depending on size	–
whole fish, small	10–20 minutes depending on size	25–40 minutes depending on size	–
whole fish, large	–	40–60 minutes	40–60 minutes
fish cakes	3–4 minutes	–	–
lobster (whole)	5–6 minutes each side	–	–
large prawns	3–4 minutes each side	–	–
small prawns	2 minutes each side	–	–

Marinades

White fish such as cod and hake has little or no fat of its own, and so marinades for this type of fish should have a little oil added to them. Oily fish like salmon and mackerel, on the other hand, do not need an oily marinade and, indeed, can manage without being marinated at all. Fish is a delicately flavoured food and if you do decide to marinate, be gentle with the extent of the flavouring.

LEMON MARINADE FOR WHITE FISH

juice of 3 lemons
3×15ml spoons/3 tablespoons cooking oil
3 shallots **or** 6 spring onions, finely chopped
1 bay leaf
1 sprig of parsley
½×2.5ml spoon/¼ teaspoon mild paprika
½×2.5ml spoon/¼ teaspoon coriander
a pinch of nutmet
½×2.5ml spoon/¼ teaspoon celery salt

Mix all the ingredients together and pour over the fish. Leave to stand for at least 1 hour.

Note This marinade can be used to baste fish towards the end of the cooking time.

WHITE WINE MARINADE FOR ANY FISH

150ml/¼ pint white wine
1 carrot, sliced
1 small onion, sliced
1 stick of celery, sliced
1×15ml spoon/1 tablespoon cooking oil
1 bay leaf
a pinch of dried thyme
black pepper

Mix all the ingredients together and pour over the fish. Leave to stand for at least 1 hour.

Note This marinade may need a little more oil added to baste the fish towards the end of the cooking time.

Barbecued Fish

FENNEL FISH STEAKS

4 thick steaks, cod, hake **or** halibut
2×15ml spoons/2 tablespoons cooking oil
1×15ml spoon/1 tablespoon lemon juice
1×5ml spoon/1 teaspoon fennel seed, crushed a little salt, black pepper

Place the fish in a shallow dish. Mix the cooking oil, lemon juice, fennel and black pepper, and pour this over the fish. Chill in a refrigerator for 2 hours.

Drain the fish, and season with salt. Grill over the barbecue for about 5–8 minutes each side, depending on thickness. Brush with a little more of the marinade as the fish cooks.

PIQUANT PRAWNS

12–16 shell-on king prawns, washed and cleaned
1 × 15ml spoon / 1 tablespoon clear honey
1 × 15ml spoon / 1 tablespoon soy sauce
4 × 15ml spoons / 4 tablespoons dry sherry
3–4 drops Tabasco sauce
a pinch of Cayenne pepper
1 × 5ml spoon / 1 teaspoon cooking oil

Place the prawns in a bowl, mix all the remaining ingredients together, and pour over the prawns. Leave in a cool place for at least 2 hours.

Drain, and place on the barbecue grill. Cook for 3–4 minutes on each side.

PORTUGUESE GRILLED SARDINES

20–30 fresh sardines, gutted, washed and wiped
2 × 15ml spoons / 2 tablespoons olive oil
2 × 15ml spoons / 2 tablespoons lemon juice
1 shallot **or** 2 spring onions, finely chopped
1 bay leaf
a pinch of dried thyme

Score each side of each fish 2–3 times with a sharp knife and place in a shallow dish. Mix the remaining ingredients together and pour over the top. Leave to stand for at least 1 hour, turning the fish from time to time.

Drain the fish, and place on a hinged fish grill which has been lightly rubbed with oil. Close the grill and place over the barbecue. Grill for 4–5 minutes on each side, brushing with a little more of the marinade towards the end of the cooking time.

Note In Portugal these sardines are always served with crispy rolls and a tomato salad.

BARBECUED TROUT

50g/2oz butter, melted
2 × 15ml spoons / 2 tablespoons lemon juice
a little grated lemon rind
1 × 15ml spoon / 1 tablespoon freshly chopped parsley
1 × 2.5ml spoon / $\frac{1}{2}$ teaspoon dried thyme
salt, freshly ground black pepper
4 trout, cleaned and washed

Mix all the ingredients except the trout. Brush the fish inside and out with the mixture and place on the grill. Cook for about 10–15 minutes, depending on the size of the trout, turning several times during cooking. Brush with a little more of the butter and lemon mixture towards the end of the cooking time. The fish is cooked when it starts to flake from the bones when tested with a fork.

CHEESY FISH PARCELS

4 thick cod, hake **or** halibut steaks
cooking oil
garlic salt, black pepper
2 tomatoes, skinned and sliced **or** 2 small courgettes, thinly sliced
50g/2oz Parmesan cheese, grated
juice of $\frac{1}{2}$ lemon
$\frac{1}{2}$ × 2.5ml spoon / $\frac{1}{4}$ teaspoon oregano

Cut aluminium foil into four pieces large enough to enwrap the steaks completely. Brush with oil. Season the fish on both sides with garlic salt and pepper. Place a fish steak on each piece of foil and arrange the sliced tomatoes or courgettes on top. Sprinkle with a little cheese, lemon juice and oregano, and close up, making sure that the parcels are completely sealed. Place on the grill and cook for about 30 minutes, depending on the thickness of the steaks.

PLAICE WITH BANANAS

2×15ml spoons/2 tablespoons cooking oil
1×15ml spoon/1 tablespoon lemon juice
salt, pepper
a pinch of dried mixed herbs
4 small whole plaice **or** dabs, washed and dried
4 bananas in their skins

Mix the cooking oil, lemon juice, seasoning and herbs. Brush the fish with this mixture. Lightly oil one or two hinged fish grills and arrange the fish in them. Place on the grill and cook for about 6–8 minutes each side, depending on the size of the fish. Brush with more of the oil and lemon mixture as required. Place the bananas in their skins on the grill at the same time, and turn from time to time. Serve the fish and the bananas together.

Variation

Fillet the fish and peel and slice the bananas. Roll up the fish fillets with the sliced bananas and wrap in oiled foil parcels with a little lemon juice, seasoning and mixed herbs. Cook on the grill for about 30 minutes until cooked through.

ORANGE BARBECUED MACKEREL

4 mackerel, cleaned and washed
3 oranges
3×15ml spoons/3 tablespoons cooking oil
salt, black pepper

Score the fish with a sharp knife at 5cm/2 inch intervals on each side. Place in a shallow dish. Peel and segment one of the oranges. Remove any tough membranes and arrange the segments inside the fish. Squeeze out the remaining oranges and grate a little of the rind off one of them. Mix the juice and rind with the cooking oil and pepper, and pour this over the fish. Leave to stand in a cool place for at least 1 hour, turning the fish once.

Grill over the barbecue in a wire mesh fish holder, and cook for 15–20 minutes, depending on the size of the fish, turning from time to time.

Orange Barbecued Mackerel and Salmon Steaks

BARBECUED MONKFISH FINGERS

2×15ml spoons/2 tablespoons concentrated tomato purée
2–3 spring onions **or** 1 shallot, very finely chopped
1×15ml spoon/1 tablespoon freshly chopped parsley
2×5ml spoons/2 teaspoons freshly chopped basil **or**
1×2.5ml spoon/½ teaspoon dried basil
a pinch of dried thyme
2×15ml spoons/2 tablespoons lemon juice
2×15ml spoons/2 tablespoons cooking oil
1×5ml spoon/1 teaspoon Worcestershire sauce
600g/1¼lb monkfish, boned and cut into pieces
10cm/4 inches×2.5cm/1 inch (approx)
salt, black pepper

Mix the tomato purée with the chopped onion and herbs, and stir in the lemon juice, half the cooking oil and the Worcestershire sauce. Spread the mixture over each piece of monkfish, and place in a bowl with any remaining marinade. Leave to stand in a cool place for at least 2 hours.

Scrape off any excess marinade, then brush the fish with a little more oil, and season to taste. Grill on the barbecue for about 3–4 minutes on each side.

FOIL BAKED FISH WITH HERBS

1 sea bass, bream or salmon trout (1.5kg/3lb approx), cleaned and washed
5–6 sprigs fresh fennel, rosemary, thyme **or** basil
75ml/3 fl oz white wine
1×15ml spoon/1 tablespoon cooking oil
1 onion, sliced
salt, freshly ground black pepper

Line a baking tray with aluminium foil just large enough to take the fish. Lay the fish in the tin and place 4–5 sprigs of your chosen herb inside. Mix together all the remaining ingredients and pour over the fish. Add the rest of the herb and leave to marinate for 3–4 hours in a refrigerator. Turn the fish once or twice during this time.

Remove the foil with the fish and marinade from the baking tray and place on the grill over the barbecue. Keep the edges of the foil turned up to stop the juices escaping. Spread out the coals under the fish and cook for about 45 minutes until the fish is tender. Baste with the juices fairly frequently.

Note Use fennel with sea bass, rosemary or basil with salmon trout, and thyme with sea bream.

COOKING ON A SKEWER

Cooking on a skewer is just as easy as any other form of barbecue cooking and the potential for variety is enormous. Any kind of food can be used, but do take relative cooking times into account when making up a new kebab. On the whole, vegetables take less time to cook than meat, so cut the meat into smaller pieces and the two should be ready together.

Basic Preparation and Cooking

Most of the meat will need to be tenderized by marinating before cooking, and fish and some vegetables will also benefit from the addition of the extra oil and moisture in a marinade. Choose suitable marinades from pages 26–7, pages 34–6 and page 50. If marinating in a refrigerator, remember to bring meat up to room temperature before cooking.

Take the food out of the marinade before grilling, and thread in an interesting manner on to the skewers. Brush with just a little oil, and cook for about 10 minutes, turning frequently. Baste with the marinade or another sauce towards the end of the cooking time. Fish kebabs may take only about 5–6 minutes to cook.

If you have a motorized rotisserie with a kebab attachment, take extra care to ensure an even load when threading the food on to the skewers. Otherwise, the kebab will strain the motor and may even just hang with the heaviest side towards the heat.

Kebabs are excellent served on rice. Alternatively, they may be enclosed in hot finger rolls or pitta bread halves. In the latter case, arrange a little shredded lettuce and onion in the cavity before adding the kebab. For plain meat kebabs, garnish with tomato quarters and black olives.

CURRIED BEEF KEBABS

600g/1¼lb lean frying steak, cut into chunks
2 small onions, quartered
150ml/¼ pint beer
1×15ml spoon/1 tablespoon mild curry powder **or** paste
1×15ml spoon/1 tablespoon concentrated tomato purée
1×15ml spoon/1 tablespoon cooking oil
1 clove of garlic, crushed (optional)
salt, black pepper

Place the steak and onions in a bowl. Mix all the remaining ingredients together and pour over the meat. Cover and chill in a refrigerator for 2–3 hours before using.

Thread on to four skewers, and grill over a hot barbecue for about 5 minutes, turning 2–3 times during cooking.

BEEF AND FENNEL KEBABS

600g/1¼lb lean frying steak, cut into chunks
4×15ml spoons/4 tablespoons yoghurt
1×15ml spoon/1 tablespoon lemon juice
1×5ml spoon/1 teaspoon cooking oil
1 bouquet garni
2 heads Italian fennel
4 tomatoes, halved

Place the beef in a bowl. Mix the yoghurt, lemon juice and cooking oil, and pour over the beef. Add the bouquet garni and leave in a cool place for 2–3 hours.

Cut the fennel in half, and blanch in a pan of boiling salted water for 6–8 minutes. Drain, and cut into pieces. Thread the beef on to skewers, alternating with pieces of fennel and adding a tomato half at each end. Grill over a hot barbecue for about 5–6 minutes, turning 2–3 times during cooking.

Serbian Minced Meat Skewers

250g/8oz lean pork, minced
250g/8oz fatty beef, minced
salt, pepper
a pinch of nutmeg
1 large onion, finely chopped
$\frac{1}{4}$–$\frac{1}{2}$ × 5ml spoon/$\frac{1}{4}$–$\frac{1}{2}$ teaspoon ground chilli powder
150ml/$\frac{1}{4}$ pint yoghurt
1 × 2.5ml spoon/$\frac{1}{2}$ teaspoon ground cumin

Mince the pork and beef 2–3 times together or chop in a food processor until very fine. Mix in plenty of seasoning and the nutmeg with a fork, and knead to a smooth paste. Shape into twelve small sausages and thread on to skewers. Leave to stand for 4–5 hours in a refrigerator and then grill over the barbecue. Allow about 10–12 minutes, turning from time to time. Test after about 8–10 minutes as it is very easy to overcook these little sausages.

Place the onion in a small bowl and sprinkle with the chilli powder. Mix the yoghurt with the cumin and serve with the kebabs in another bowl as an accompaniment.

Meatballs on a Stick

600g/1$\frac{1}{4}$lb minced steak
salt, pepper

COATINGS FOR 4 MEATBALLS EACH
1 × 15ml spoon/1 tablespoon very finely chopped parsley
1 × 15ml spoon/1 tablespoon very finely chopped mint
1 × 15ml spoon/1 tablespoon sesame seeds
1 × 15ml spoon/1 tablespoon poppyseeds
2 × 5ml spoons/2 teaspoons paprika
1 × 15ml spoon/1 tablespoon coarsely ground black pepper

Season the meat and shape into 16 balls. Roll each ball in one of the coatings, making sure that the meat is completely covered and that the coating is pressed as well. Thread four balls on to each skewer, and grill over the barbecue for 7–8 minutes, turning from time to time.

Meatballs on a Stick

TIKKA KEBABS

½ leg of lamb (1kg/2lb approx), boned and cut into
chunks
4×15ml spoons/4 tablespoons yoghurt
2 large cloves garlic, crushed
1.25cm/½inch piece of fresh root ginger, grated
1×5ml spoon/1 teaspoon ground cumin
salt, pepper
1 lemon, quartered
1 onion, cut into rings
a pinch of chilli powder

Place the meat in a large basin. Mix the yoghurt with the garlic, ginger, cumin and seasoning, and pour over the meat. Leave to marinate for 3–4 hours or overnight. Stir from time to time.

Thread the meat on to four skewers, and grill over the barbecue for about 15 minutes, turning 2–3 times. Serve with lemon quarters and with onion rings sprinkled with chilli powder.

LAMB, MUSHROOM AND KIDNEY KEBABS

4 lamb's kidneys, halved
500g/1lb shoulder **or** fillet of lamb, boned, cut into
chunks and marinated (see **Note**)
2 onions, quartered
100g/4oz button mushrooms
salt, pepper
cooking oil

Thread the kidney and lamb on to skewers, alternating with the onions and mushrooms. Season to taste, and brush with oil. Grill over the barbecue for about 15 minutes, turning 2–3 times.

Note Marinate the lamb for this recipe in one of the marinades listed for lamb on pages 34–6.

SOSATIES

½ leg of lamb (1kg/2lb approx), boned and cut into
chunks
300ml/½pint vinegar
150ml/¼pint water
2×15ml spoons/2 tablespoons apricot jam
1×15ml spoon/1 tablespoon curry powder
1×15ml spoon/1 tablespoon turmeric
1×15ml spoon/1 tablespoon sugar
500g/1lb onions, cut into chunks
250g/8oz dried apricots
2 cloves garlic, crushed
1 bay leaf

Place the meat in a large pan. Put all the remaining ingredients into a saucepan, and bring to the boil. Remove from the heat and leave to cool. Pour over the meat and marinate for 2–3 days in a refrigerator.

Thread the pieces of lamb, onion and apricots on to skewers, and grill over the barbecue for about 15 minutes, turning once or twice during cooking.

LAMB WITH PEPPERS

500g/1lb shoulder of lamb, boned and cut into chunks
juice of 1 lemon
cooking oil
4 small onions, cut into quarters
1 green pepper, de-seeded and cut into pieces
1 red pepper, de-seeded and cut into pieces
salt and pepper

Marinate the lamb in a little lemon juice and oil for about 1 hour. Thread the meat on to skewers, alternating with the onion quarters and pieces of pepper. Sprinkle with salt and pepper, and grill over the barbecue for about 15 minutes, turning 2–3 times during cooking.

Veal and Mushroom Kebabs with Rosemary

600g/1¼ lb pie veal, cut into chunks
175g/6oz button mushrooms, stalks removed
150ml/¼ pint medium-dry white wine
2×15ml spoons/2 tablespoons cooking oil
1 carrot, sliced
1 very small onion **or** 2 shallots, sliced
1 stick of celery, sliced
4 sprigs fresh rosemary **or** 1×5ml spoon/1 teaspoon
dried rosemary
freshly ground black pepper

Put the veal and mushrooms into a bowl. Mix the wine and oil and pour over the top. Add the vegetables, herbs and black pepper. Leave to stand in a cool place for at least 2 hours.

Drain the meat and mushrooms, and thread on to skewers. Brush lightly with a little more cooking oil, and grill for about 12–14 minutes, turning frequently during cooking.

Chicken and Lamb Satay

½ large fresh chicken
1×15ml spoon/1 tablespoon concentrated tomato purée
salt, pepper
300g/10oz lamb fillet, cut into small chunks
2×15ml spoons/2 tablespoons soy sauce

Cut the flesh from the bones and cut the chicken into small chunks. Place in a bowl, and mix with the tomato purée and seasoning. Chill in a refrigerator for 2 hours. Mix the lamb with the soy sauce and leave to stand with the chicken.

Thread the meat on to small wooden skewers, keeping each meat separate. Grill on the barbecue for about 12–15 minutes, turning regularly. Serve with Satay Sauce (page 66).

Chicken and Pineapple Kebabs

1 large fresh chicken
3×15ml spoons/3 tablespoons yoghurt
3–4 sprigs fresh mint, freshly chopped
1×5ml spoon/1 teaspoon vinegar
salt, pepper
250g/8oz fresh **or** canned pineapple rings
2 small green peppers, de-seeded and cut into pieces

Cut the flesh from the bones and cut the chicken into large chunks. Place in a bowl. Mix the yoghurt, mint, vinegar and seasoning, and pour over the chicken. Mix well and chill for 3–4 hours, stirring from time to time.

To make up the skewers, cut the pineapple rings into chunks, and thread on to skewers, alternating with pieces of green pepper and chunks of marinated chicken. Grill on the barbecue for 15–20 minutes, turning at least three times during cooking.

Sausage and Prune Kebabs

4 German bratwurst sausages
8 dried prunes, soaked overnight
4 small onions, skinned and quartered

Cut each sausage into six pieces. Drain the prunes, and thread three pieces of sausage, two quarters of onion and two prunes on to each skewer. Grill for about 6–8 minutes, turning from time to time.

SPICY SAUSAGE KEBABS

500g/1 lb chipolata sausages
100g/4 oz streaky bacon, without rinds
50–75g/2–3 oz button mushrooms
cooking oil
salt, pepper

BASTING SAUCE
2×15ml spoons/2 tablespoons dry cider
2×15ml spoons/2 tablespoons clear honey
1×5ml spoon/1 teaspoon tomato ketchup
3–4 drops Tabasco sauce
juice of ½ lemon

Twist the sausages in the middle, and cut in half. Stretch each bacon rasher by rubbing with the back of a knife. Cut in half and wrap each rasher round a mushroom. Thread the sausages and mushrooms alternately along the skewers. Brush with oil, then season to taste. Set over the barbecue to start cooking.

Meanwhile, prepare the sauce, or prepare the sauce in advance. Place all the ingredients in a saucepan and bring to the boil. Use to brush the kebabs as they continue to cook. Spoon a little extra sauce over each kebab as it is served.

SCALLOP SKEWERS

500g/1 lb scallops
½ cucumber, cut into large cubes
a few sprigs fresh thyme
cooking oil
salt, pepper

Cut the scallops in half and thread on to skewers with the cucumber and thyme. Brush lightly with oil, then season to taste. Place on the barbecue, and grill for 6–8 minutes, turning from time to time. Serve with wedges of lemon.

MINTED PRAWNS

6–8 sprigs fresh mint **or** 1×5ml spoon/1 teaspoon dried mint
juice of 1 lemon
250g/8 oz shell-on prawns (24 approx), washed and cleaned

Crush 3–4 sprigs of fresh mint in the lemon juice until it runs green, or mix in the dried mint. Pour the mixture over the prawns, and leave to stand in a cool place for 2 hours.

Thread the prawns on to skewers alternating with the remaining mint sprigs, and grill for about 2 minutes on each side. Do not cook for too long; the prawns only need to be heated through, and excessive grilling will harden the flesh.

SKEWERED SPRATS

16–20 sprats
4×15ml spoons/4 tablespoons soy sauce
juice of 2 lemons
cooking oil
salt, pepper

Prick the sprats along their backs with a fork. Place in a shallow dish and pour the soy sauce and lemon juice over the top. Leave to stand in a cool place for at least 1 hour.

Drain the fish and run a skewer through the head and tail of each, allowing about 4–5 sprats to each skewer. Brush lightly with cooking oil, and season well. Cook over the grill for 8–10 minutes, turning from time to time.

Minted Prawns and *Vegetable Kebabs* (page 63)

Varied Vegetables

Vegetables can be cooked on the barbecue on skewers, or they can be wrapped in foil or even cooked in their own skins and placed in the embers or on the grill. If you are spit-roasting, vegetables can be cooked in the drip tray.

Basic Preparation

Aubergines: Cut into cubes and sprinkle with salt. Leave to stand for 1 hour. Rinse under cold water and use on skewers.

Courgettes: Wash and cut into chunks. Use small courgettes without blanching but blanch larger vegetables for 1 minute in boiling water.

Green peppers: De-seed and cut into chunky pieces. Blanch by plunging into boiling water for 1 minute, then drain and cool. This helps to prevent splitting on the skewer.

Mushrooms: Wash and remove the stalks. Soak in a marinade, or blanch for 1 minute in boiling water.

Onions: Small onions can be skewered whole. Skin the onion and cook in boiling water for 5 minutes before skewering. Pieces of onion can be cooked on the skewer. Avoid cutting the onion into rings as this can be very difficult to keep on the skewer.

Tomatoes: Choose small tomatoes and use whole or halved. Smaller sections tend to fall off the skewer as the vegetable cooks.

When cooking vegetables in foil, remember to arrange the foil with the dull side outside to reduce the risk of burning.

Baked Potatoes

4 large potatoes
butter **or** soured cream
chopped chives

Scrub the potatoes, and prick all over with a fork. Double-wrap in foil and bake on the coals for 1 hour. Alternatively, parboil for 10–15 minutes or bake in the oven at 180°C/350°F/Gas 4 for 30 minutes. Drain or remove from the oven and place on the barbecue grill for a further 30 minutes until soft.

Stuff with butter or with soured cream mixed with chives.

Barbecued Onions

4 medium onions

Leave the skins intact and place on the grill. Turn from time to time. The onions will be cooked in about 45 minutes, depending on size.

Alternatively, skin the onions, and wrap in double-thickness foil. Cook on the coals for about 1 hour.

Barbecued Sweetcorn

4 heads sweetcorn
salt
butter

Fold back the husks from the corn and cut out the cob, retaining the husk. Remove the silky hairs, and cook in lightly salted boiling water for 5 minutes. (With very fresh corn this pre-cooking can be omitted.) Return the cob to the husk, and grill over the barbecue for about 30 minutes.

Alternatively, wrap the pre-cooked cob in buttered double-thickness foil, and grill for 30–40 minutes.

Vegetable Kebabs

100g/4oz button mushrooms, stalks removed
2×15ml spoons/2 tablespoons cooking oil
juice of ½ lemon
3 small courgettes, each cut into 4 chunks
8 small tomatoes

Put the mushrooms in a basin, and pour the cooking oil and lemon juice over the top. Leave to stand for an hour or so, turning the mushrooms from time to time.

Thread the mushrooms, courgette pieces and tomatoes on to four skewers. Brush with a little of the mushroom marinade, and grill over the barbecue for 10–15 minutes, turning from time to time. Brush with more of the marinade as required.

Vegetable Parcels

375g/12oz green peas
250g/8oz sweetcorn kernels
1 green pepper, very finely chopped
1 red pepper, very finely chopped
4 knobs butter
salt, freshly ground black pepper

Cut aluminium foil into four squares. Divide the vegetables between the foil. Top with a knob of butter, and season to taste. Wrap up into four parcels, making sure that they are well sealed. Cook over the barbecue for about 20–30 minutes.

Baked Chestnuts

500g/1lb chestnuts

Make two slits in each of the chestnuts, and wrap up in foil parcels. Place in the coals to cook, and leave for about 45 minutes.

Stuffed Mushrooms

8 large field mushrooms
2×15ml spoons/2 tablespoons fresh breadcrumbs
4 spring onions, finely chopped
1 tomato, skinned and chopped
1×5ml spoon/1 teaspoon concentrated tomato purée
1×5ml spoon/1 teaspoon lemon juice
1×2.5ml spoon/½ teaspoon dried thyme
salt, freshly ground black pepper

Cut the stalks off the mushrooms and chop very finely. Mix with all the remaining ingredients and pile back on to the mushrooms. Press well down. Arrange the mushrooms on a double layer of buttered aluminium foil with the dull side facing the coals. Cook for about 5–6 minutes.

ACCOMPANIMENTS

The various accompaniments to a barbecue can be almost as important as the meat or fish for grilling. Everyone always seems to eat more in the open air, so a good selection of side salads, fillers such as bread, potatoes and rice dishes all help to fill in the gaps, and punches, mulled wine and other drinks will most certainly add to the festive atmosphere.

Butters and Sauces

Plainly grilled meat and fish taste really good from the barbecue. However, such relatively plain fare does need an interesting sauce or a savoury butter to draw out the flavour. Two or three sauces and butters per party will provide a good selection for your guests.

BARBECUE BUTTER

100g/4oz butter, softened
1×5ml spoon/1 teaspoon dry mustard
1 clove of garlic, crushed
1×5ml spoon/1 teaspoon concentrated tomato purée
salt, pepper

Cream the butter and gradually add the mustard, making sure that no lumps of dry powder remain in the mixture. Beat in the garlic, then the tomato purée and the salt and pepper. Spread the butter mixture 5mm/¼ inch thick on a piece of greaseproof paper, and chill in a refrigerator until set. When it is really hard, stamp the butter into rounds with a small pastry cutter. Serve on grilled steaks, lamb chops and gammon rounds.

LEMON BUTTER

100g/4oz butter, softened
1×5ml spoon/1 teaspoon grated lemon rind
1×2.5ml spoon/½ teaspoon dried mixed herbs
salt, pepper

Cream the butter and beat in the remaining ingredients. Spread 5mm/¼ inch thick on a piece of greaseproof paper, and chill in a refrigerator until set. When it is really hard, stamp the butter into rounds with a small pastry cutter. Serve on grilled lamb chops, chicken and steaks.

GARLIC BUTTER

100g/4oz butter, softened
1×15ml spoon/1 tablespoon freshly chopped parsley
2 cloves garlic, very finely chopped

Cream the butter with the parsley and garlic. Spread 5mm/
$\frac{1}{4}$ inch thick on a piece of greaseproof paper, and chill in a refrigerator until set. When it is really hard, stamp the butter into rounds with a small pastry cutter. Serve on grilled lamb, beef or fish.

MAÎTRE D'HÔTEL BUTTER

100g/4oz butter, softened
1×15ml spoon/1 tablespoon freshly chopped parsley
salt, freshly ground black pepper
a dash of lemon juice

Cream the butter and beat in the remaining ingredients to a smooth paste. Spread 5mm/$\frac{1}{4}$ inch thick on a piece of grease-proof paper, and chill in a refrigerator until set. When it is really hard, stamp the butter into rounds with a small pastry cutter. Serve on steaks and chops.
Alternatively, serve melted in a small heated jug.

BEER AND MUSTARD SAUCE

1 onion, finely chopped
1×15ml spoon/1 tablespoon cooking oil
1×15ml spoon/1 tablespoon French mustard
150ml/$\frac{1}{4}$ pint Guinness **or** brown ale
2×15ml spoons/2 tablespoons clear honey
juice of $\frac{1}{2}$ lemon
salt, pepper

Gently fry the onion in cooking oil for 5 minutes. Add all the remaining ingredients and bring to the boil. Reduce the heat and simmer for 5 minutes. Serve hot.

SWEET AND SOUR SAUCE

1 banana
juice of 1 lemon
1×15ml spoon/1 tablespoon wine vinegar
1×15ml spoon/1 tablespoon French mustard
2.5cm/1 inch fresh root ginger **or** a piece of preserved stem ginger, finely chopped
300g/10oz canned crushed pineapple

Mash the banana with a fork and mix with lemon juice to prevent it discoloring. Add the vinegar, mustard, ginger and the canned pineapple. Mix well together and serve hot or cold.

CUMBERLAND SAUCE

rind and juice of 1 orange
250g/8oz redcurrant jelly
1×5ml spoon/1 teaspoon mild made mustard
50ml/2floz port **or** red wine
juice of $\frac{1}{2}$ lemon
2–3 finely chopped shallots

Place the orange rind in boiling water for 3–4 minutes. Drain and rinse under cold water. Cut into very thin strips and put on one side. Put the redcurrant jelly in a bowl with the mustard, and whisk in the port or wine, and the strained lemon and orange juice. Add the shallots and orange strips, and serve cold.

SPICY BARBECUE SAUCE

150ml/$\frac{1}{4}$pint tomato ketchup
50ml/2floz cider vinegar
1×5ml spoon/1 teaspoon sugar
flesh of $\frac{1}{2}$ small lemon, finely chopped
1×5ml spoon/1 teaspoon ground coriander
1×2.5ml spoon/$\frac{1}{2}$ teaspoon cumin
$\frac{1}{2}$×2.5ml spoon/$\frac{1}{4}$ teaspoon ground ginger
$\frac{1}{4}$×2.5ml spoon/$\frac{1}{8}$ teaspoon paprika
salt, black pepper

Place all the ingredients in a pan, stir well and bring to the boil. Reduce the heat and simmer for 10 minutes, stirring occasionally. Serve hot or cold.

SATAY SAUCE

1 large clove of garlic
2×5ml spoons/2 teaspoons cooking oil
3×15ml spoons/3 tablespoons smooth peanut butter
50g/2oz creamed coconut
a pinch of chilli powder
juice of $\frac{1}{2}$ lemon
1×15ml spoon/1 tablespoon soy sauce
3–4×15ml spoons/3–4 tablespoons chicken stock

Gently fry the garlic in the oil for 1–2 minutes. Add the peanut butter and coconut, and stir until the coconut melts. Add all the remaining ingredients except the fruit, and stir over low heat. As the mixture comes to the boil it will thicken to the consistency of whipped cream. Remove from the heat, and serve. If the sauce becomes thick, simply add a little more stock.

Variation
Serve the sauce in the centre of 8 peach halves or pineapple rings, with any remaining sauce in a small bowl.

MUSHROOM SAUCE

15g/$\frac{1}{2}$oz butter
250g/8oz button mushrooms, finely chopped
15g/$\frac{1}{2}$oz plain flour
300ml/$\frac{1}{2}$pint chicken stock
1×5ml spoon/1 teaspoon Worcestershire sauce
1×2.5ml spoon/$\frac{1}{2}$ teaspoon garlic salt
a pinch of dried thyme
freshly ground black pepper

Melt the butter in a pan. Gently fry the mushrooms in the melted butter for 2–3 minutes until softened. Stir in the flour and then the chicken stock. Bring to the boil and cook for 1–2 minutes, stirring all the time. Add the Worcestershire sauce, garlic salt, thyme and black pepper, and cook for a further 1–2 minutes. Serve hot.

Side salads are always welcome at outdoor parties, and particularly as a contrast to the hot food eaten with them. Two or three salads per party is quite adequate.

SALISBURY SALAD

1 small lettuce
1 large head of chicory, sliced
50g/2oz button mushrooms, sliced
4×15ml spoons/4 tablespoons bean sprouts
4×15ml spoons/4 tablespoons yoghurt
1×2.5ml spoon/½ teaspoon dried thyme
salt, pepper
2 large tomatoes, sliced

Tear the lettuce into pieces and mix in a large bowl with the sliced chicory, mushrooms and bean sprouts. Mix the yoghurt, thyme and seasoning, and spoon half the mixture into the salad. Toss again. Arrange the sliced tomatoes around the top. Spoon the remaining yoghurt into the centre, and serve.

AMERICAN FRUIT SLAW

1 eating apple, coarsely grated and mixed with juice of
½ lemon
1 large carrot, coarsely grated
1 green pepper, de-seeded and cut into very thin slices
175g/6oz white cabbage, finely shredded
2×15ml spoons/2 tablespoons mayonnaise
1×2.5ml spoon/½ teaspoon mild French mustard
black pepper

Mix together the apple and carrot and then mix in the green pepper and cabbage. Mix the mayonnaise with the mustard and pepper, and add to the bowl. Toss all the ingredients well together.

BARBECUE SALAD

1 avocado pear
juice of ½ lemon
3 tomatoes, chopped
4 large sticks celery, chopped
½ small head fennel, chopped
5cm/2 inches cucumber, cubed
½ large green pepper, de-seeded and chopped
6 cos lettuce leaves, shredded
2×15ml spoons/2 tablespoons raisins
3×15ml spoons/3 tablespoons salad oil
1×5ml spoon/1 teaspoon wine vinegar
1×2.5ml spoon/½ teaspoon French mustard
black pepper

Halve, stone and peel the avocado pear. Cut into small pieces and toss in some lemon juice. Drain, and retain the juice. Add all the remaining vegetables and the raisins to the bowl. Mix the reserved lemon juice with the oil, vinegar, mustard and pepper. Pour over the salad and toss well together.

HOT POTATO SALAD

500g/1lb small red skinned **or** new potatoes
50ml/2fl oz white wine
4 spring onions, finely chopped
1×15ml spoon/1 tablespoon olive oil
chopped parsley

Boil or steam the potatoes in their skins until just tender. Put the wine and onions in a large bowl and stand the bowl over a pan of boiling water. Peel the potatoes and add to the wine in the bowl. Cut into pieces if the potatoes are very large. When the wine has heated through, add the olive oil, sprinkle with chopped parsley, and serve.

RICE AND BEAN SALAD

250g/8oz broad beans
salt
100g/4oz long grain rice
200ml/8fl oz chicken stock
2–3×15ml spoons/2–3 tablespoons oil and vinegar
dressing
100g/4oz salted peanuts

Cook the beans in salted water until tender. Put the rice, salt and stock in a pan and bring to the boil. Stir, cover and simmer for 12–15 minutes until the rice is tender and all the liquid has been absorbed. Leave to cool a little and mix with the oil and vinegar dressing. When completely cold, stir in the beans and peanuts, and season to taste.

SWEET AND SOUR SALAD

juice of ½ lemon
juice of ½ orange
1×5ml spoon/1 teaspoon wine or cider vinegar
1×15ml spoon/1 tablespoon olive oil
a pinch of sugar
salt, pepper
1 large ripe pear, peeled, cored and diced
centre of 1 head of celery, chopped
5cm/2 inches cucumber, chopped
½ bunch watercress
25g/1oz dry roasted peanuts

Mix the fruit juices with the vinegar, oil, sugar and seasoning, and place in a bowl. Add the pear, making sure that it is well covered with the dressing. Mix in the celery and cucumber. Arrange the watercress on the top, leaving a space in the centre. Sprinkle this space with the nuts, and serve at once.

SPINACH AND BACON SALAD

75g/3oz streaky bacon, without rinds
175g/6oz fresh young spinach, washed and drained
2×15ml spoons/2 tablespoons olive or salad oil
2×15ml spoons/2 tablespoons dry sherry
black pepper

Grill the bacon until crisp. Cool, then cut into small pieces. Put the spinach in a large bowl and sprinkle with the bacon. Mix all the remaining ingredients and pour over the salad.

PROVENÇALE COURGETTE SALAD

500g/1lb small courgettes, finely sliced
4 large tomatoes, peeled and chopped
4 spring onions or shallots, finely chopped
3×15ml spoons/3 tablespoons freshly chopped parsley
½ small lettuce, shredded
3×15ml spoons/3 tablespoons salad oil
2×15ml spoons/2 tablespoons tomato juice
1×15ml spoon/1 tablespoon lemon juice
1 clove of garlic, crushed
1×2.5ml spoon/½ teaspoon fennel seed
½×2.5ml spoon/¼ teaspoon dried thyme
a pinch of dried rosemary
black pepper

Mix the courgettes, tomatoes, spring onions or shallots and parsley in a bowl. Line a salad bowl with the lettuce, and top with the courgette mixture. Mix all the remaining ingredients to make a dressing, and pour over the top.

A Selection of Accompaniments
Provençale Courgette Salad, *Rice and Bean Salad* and *Garlic Bread (page 70)*

Fillers

Baskets of French bread and rolls and other fillers all help to stem the immense outdoor hunger created by the barbecue aroma.

BARBECUED BREAD CRISPS

4×15ml spoons/4 tablespoons cooking oil
1×15ml spoon/1 tablespoon tomato ketchup
1×5ml spoon/1 teaspoon Worcestershire sauce
1×5ml spoon/1 teaspoon concentrated tomato purée
1×5ml spoon/1 teaspoon herb flavoured mustard
4–5 large slices white bread

Mix all the ingredients except the bread, and beat well with a fork. Spread liberally over both sides of the bread with a pastry brush. Place on a baking tray and bake at 230°C/450°F/Gas 8 for about 10–15 minutes until crisp and brown. Cut into triangles and serve at once, or leave to cool and re-heat quickly over the barbecue.

Note These spicy bread crisps make a good appetizer or they can be served with the barbecue itself.

TEXAS TOAST

100g/4oz butter, melted
1–2 cloves garlic, crushed
8 slices thickly sliced toast

Mix the butter and garlic, and brush both sides of each slice of toast with the mixture. Lay the buttered toast directly on the oven shelves and bake at 180°C/350°F/Gas 4 for 5–8 minutes until golden.

GARLIC OR HERB AND LEMON BREAD

1 French loaf

GARLIC FILLING
100g/4oz butter, softened
1×15ml spoon/1 tablespoon freshly chopped parsley
2 cloves garlic, very finely chopped

or

HERB AND LEMON FILLING
100g/4oz butter, softened
grated rind of 1 lemon
1×2.5ml spoon/½ teaspoon dried mixed herbs
1×15ml spoon/1 tablespoon freshly chopped parsley
2×5ml spoons/2 teaspoons freshly chopped chives **or** spring onions

Slice the bread at 2.5cm/1 inch intervals to within 5mm/¼ inch of the base of the loaf, so that each slice is still attached to the others.

To prepare the filling, beat the butter with the parsley and garlic or with the lemon rind, herbs, parsley and chives or onions. Use the mixture to spread over each slice of bread. Wrap the loaf in foil and place over the hottest part of the barbecue. Bake for about 10–15 minutes, turning from time to time. Open up the foil and serve with barbecued meat or fish.

DAMPERS

500g/1lb plain flour
1 × 5ml spoon / 1 teaspoon salt
1 × 5ml spoon / 1 teaspoon bicarbonate of soda
75g/3oz butter
150ml/¼ pint buttermilk **or** sour milk

Sift the flour, salt and bicarbonate of soda into a mixing bowl. Cut the butter into small pieces and rub into the flour until the mixture resembles fine breadcrumbs. Mix to a firm dough with the milk. Knead very lightly for a couple of minutes and shape into eight flattish cakes. Cook slowly over the coolest area of the barbecue for 15–20 minutes, turning once or twice during the cooking time. Serve hot with butter.

SPICED RICE

2 × 15ml spoons / 2 tablespoons whole cumin seed
2 × 15ml spoons / 2 tablespoons cooking oil
1 large onion, finely chopped
1 × 5ml spoon / 1 teaspoon ground turmeric
1 × 2.5ml spoon / ½ teaspoon ground cardamon
a pinch of cinnamon
a little grated lemon rind
250g/8oz long grain rice
salt, black pepper
2 × 15ml spoons / 2 tablespoons freshly chopped parsley
½ × 2.5ml spoon / ¼ teaspoon mixed dried herbs
475ml/16fl oz water

Fry the whole cumin seed in cooking oil for 1 minute. Add the onion and continue frying for 2–3 minutes. Add the rest of the spices, the lemon rind and the rice. Stir until the rice is fully coated with oil, then add all the remaining ingredients. Bring to the boil, reduce the heat, cover, and simmer for 15 minutes until all the liquid has been absorbed and the rice is tender. Fluff up with a fork, and serve.

BUTTERED NOODLES WITH FRESH HERBS

375g/12oz egg **or** spinach noodles
salt, black pepper
25g/1oz butter
2 × 15ml spoons / 2 tablespoons freshly chopped parsley, chervil **or** basil
1 × 5ml spoon / 1 teaspoon freshly chopped rosemary

Cook the noodles in boiling salted water for about 8–10 minutes until just tender. Drain very well and return to the pan with the butter, herbs and black pepper. Toss well together and serve at once.

LEMON POTATOES

1kg/2lb firm potatoes
100g/4oz butter
100g/4oz sugar
1 × 15ml spoon / 1 tablespoon lemon juice
1 × 5ml spoon / 1. teaspoon dried basil
grated rind of 1 lemon

Parboil the potatoes in salted water for about 8–10 minutes, then peel and slice thickly. Melt the butter and sugar in a large heavy-based frying pan, and stir in the lemon juice and basil. Continue heating until the mixture begins to bubble. Add the potatoes, and continue cooking over low heat for about 10 minutes until the potatoes are properly cooked through. Spoon the syrup over the potatoes throughout the cooking time. Sprinkle with lemon rind, and serve hot.

Drinks

The drinks are an integral part of any party and barbecues are no exception. Wine, beer and cider all go well with the informal atmosphere and outdoor setting but it is fun to make up your own cups and punches. However, if you feel like starting with a potent punch, remember that the evening could be a long one, so have something less alcoholic to follow on. A non-alcoholic cup is also welcomed by those who have to drive home. Serve the drinks in long glasses.

CIDER PUNCH

2 lemons
2 oranges
150ml/¼ pint water
75g/3 oz sugar
1 litre/1⅔ pints dry cider
75ml/3 fl oz brandy
orange slices
cucumber slices

Thinly pare the rind from the lemons and one of the oranges. Simmer in the water for about 5 minutes. Add the sugar, and stir until it has all dissolved. Strain and leave to cool.

Squeeze the juice from the pared fruit and mix with the cooled syrup. Slice the remaining orange. Put the fruit mixture, orange and cucumber slices, the cider and brandy into a bowl or jug, and stir. Serve in ice-filled glasses decorated with orange and cucumber slices.

FRUITY PUNCH

1.5 litres/2½ pints red wine, chilled
200ml/8 fl oz vodka
1 × 15ml spoon/1 tablespoon lime juice
ice cubes
1 lime **or** lemon, sliced
1 kiwi fruit, peeled and sliced
750ml/1¼ pints sparkling wine **or** 1 litre/1⅔ pints lemonade

Pour the red wine, vodka and lime juice into a large punch bowl. Add the ice cubes and fruit. Just before serving, add the sparkling wine or, for a less alcoholic follow-up, the lemonade.

Note Serves eight people with two glasses each

BARBECUE FIZZ

750ml/1¼ pints Dubonnet
200ml/8 fl oz gin
juice of 1 lemon
ice cubes
1 lemon, sliced
2 litres/3½ pints lemonade
cocktail cherries

Pour the Dubonnet and gin into a bowl and stir in the lemon juice, ice cubes and sliced lemon. Just before serving, add the lemonade. Serve with a cocktail cherry in each glass.

Note Serves eight people with two glasses each

Cider Punch and *Raspberry Fruit Punch* (page 75)

SANGRIA

750ml/1¼ pints red wine
50ml/2 fl oz brandy
50ml/2 fl oz Cointreau
juice of 1 lemon
1 orange, sliced
1 lemon, sliced
1 apple, sliced
600ml/1 pint soda water
ice cubes

Mix all the ingredients except the soda water and ice in a bowl or jug, and leave to stand for 30 minutes. Just before serving, add the soda water and ice cubes.

Variation
Use Anis instead of Cointreau for a change of flavour.

MINT JULEP

1½ × 15ml spoons/1½ tablespoons sugar
4 × 15ml spoons/4 tablespoons water
6–8 sprigs mint
crushed ice
200ml/8 fl oz bourbon whisky

Dissolve the sugar in the water and add 2–3 sprigs of mint. Bruise with a wooden spoon until the syrup is green in colour. Fill up a small jug with crushed ice, and pour in the mint syrup and the bourbon whisky. Chill in a refrigerator for 30–40 minutes before serving in frosted glasses. Decorate each glass with the remaining sprigs of mint.

COLOMBO COOLER

25ml/1 fl oz gin
25ml/1 fl oz sweet white vermouth
ice cubes
300ml/½ pint dry ginger ale
cocktail cherry

Pour the gin and vermouth into a tall glass and add the ice cubes. Top up with ginger ale, and decorate with a cocktail cherry.

Note Serves one

OLD FASHIONED PUNCH

25ml/1 fl oz rum
1 × 5ml spoon/1 teaspoon fresh lemon juice
1 × 5ml spoon/1 teaspoon lime juice
a dash of Angostura bitters
ice cubes
soda water
a slice of lemon
a sprig of borage

Pour the rum into a tall glass and add the lemon and lime juices, the bitters and ice cubes. Top up with soda water, and decorate with a lemon slice and a sprig of borage.

Note Serves one

SPARKLING WINE CUP

1.5 litres/2½ pints sparkling white wine, well chilled
100ml/4fl oz brandy
2×5ml spoons/2 teaspoons grenadine
ice cubes
250g/8oz fresh strawberries

Pour the wine into a bowl, and stir in the brandy, grenadine and ice cubes. Float the strawberries on the top.

HOT MULLED WINE

300ml/½ pint water
2 cinnamon sticks
4 cloves
1 lemon
1×15ml spoon/1 tablespoon sugar
3×15ml spoons/3 tablespoons brandy
1.5 litres/2½ pints red wine

Pour the water in a saucepan with the cinnamon sticks. Stick the cloves into the lemon, and add to the pan. Bring the water to the boil, and simmer for 10 minutes. Strain, and return to a larger pan with the sugar. Stir until all the sugar has dissolved. Stir in the brandy and red wine, and heat gently. Do not allow to boil. Serve hot.

WEST COUNTRY CUP

1 litre/1⅔ pints apple juice, chilled
juice of 2 lemons
1×5ml spoon/1 teaspoon grenadine
ice cubes
1 red apple, sliced
1 green apple, sliced
1 litre/1⅔ pints sparkling water, chilled

Pour the apple juice and lemon juice into a bowl and add the grenadine, ice cubes and fruit. Just before serving, pour in the chilled sparkling water.

RASPBERRY FRUIT PUNCH

600ml/1 pint grapefruit juice
3×15ml spoons/3 tablespoons blackcurrant juice cordial
juice of 2 fresh lemons
750ml/1¼ pints sparkling water, chilled
1 lemon, sliced
fresh raspberries

Mix the grapefruit juice with the cordial and lemon juice in a bowl, and chill for at least 1 hour in a refrigerator. Just before serving, stir in the chilled water, and float the raspberries on top. Serve in tall glasses, each decorated with a cocktail stick carrying a slice of lemon and raspberries.

FIZZY LIZZY

600ml/1 pint pineapple juice, chilled
a dash of grenadine
1 orange, sliced
ice cubes
1 litre/1⅔ pints ginger beer, chilled

Pour the pineapple juice into a jug and add the grenadine, sliced orange and ice. Just before serving, stir in the ginger beer.

DESSERTS TO FINISH

The question of dessert cannot be ignored at a barbecue. The answer could be some barbecued fruit but it might also be a creamy mousse or a mouthwatering flan. Whatever it is, it can usually be made in advance and produced with a flourish at the end of the meal.

Barbecued Desserts

Most fruit can be cooked over the barbecue and this is quite a good way of extracting the maximum use from the dying coals. Kebabs and foil parcels are usually the best ways to cook fruit but bananas can be cooked in their own skins. And as a final touch of delicious luxury, pass round a bowl of marshmallows and some long sticks, and let your guests toast them over the last bit of heat from the coals.

BARBECUED APPLES

4 small cooking apples
4×15ml spoons/4 tablespoons dark brown sugar
2×15ml spoons/2 tablespoons raisins
a little grated lemon rind

Core the apples and cut a ring all the way round each one with a knife. Mix all the remaining ingredients together and stuff into the cored centres of the apples. Wrap each apple in foil with the shiny side of the foil against the apple. Make sure that there are no holes for the sugar and apple juices to run out. Place on the barbecue, and cook for about 40 minutes, turning from time to time. Take care when opening the parcels.

FRUIT KEBABS

Almost any kind of fruit can be used for fruit kebabs. Here are two simple combinations to try:

(1)
2 pears, peeled, cored and cut into chunks
juice of 2 lemons
2 bananas
12–16 strawberries
3×15ml spoons/3 tablespoons sugar

Place the pears in a bowl with the lemon juice to stop discolouring. Peel and cut the bananas into chunks and add to the bowl. Pick over the strawberries and add to the bowl with half the sugar. Leave to stand for 30 minutes.
Thread the fruit on to skewers. Roll in the remaining sugar, and cook over the barbecue for about 5–6 minutes, turning as the sugar caramelizes.

(2)
8–12 ripe apricots, halved and stoned
juice of 1 orange
2 eating apples, peeled, cored and cut into chunks
juice of 1 lemon
12 large grapes
2×15ml spoons/2 tablespoons sugar

Soak the halved apricots in orange juice and the apples in lemon juice for at least 30 minutes.
Thread the fruit on to skewers with the grapes. Roll the fruit kebabs in sugar, and cook over the barbecue for about 5–6 minutes, turning as the sugar caramelizes.

Melon Fruit Salad (page 79), Rich Chocolate Mousse (page 78) and Orange and Kiwi Cream Flan (page 79)

GRILLED PINEAPPLE RINGS WITH KIRSCH

1 large fresh pineapple
4×15ml spoons/4 tablespoons apricot jam
2×15ml spoons/2 tablespoons kirsch

Cut the pineapple into eight slices. Cut off the skin and cut out the hard centre. Spread each side of each slice with apricot jam. Place on a large plate, and sprinkle with kirsch. Grill over the barbecue for about 3–4 minutes on each side until the jam begins to bubble and brown.

BARBECUED BANANA FLAMBÉ

4 ripe bananas in their skins
2×15ml spoons/2 tablespoons dark brown sugar
6×15ml spoons/6 tablespoons dark rum

Grill the bananas in their skins over the barbecue for 10 minutes on each side. Cut each banana in half lengthways and sprinkle first with sugar and then with rum. Set the rum alight, and serve at once with cream or ice cream.

Non-Barbecued Desserts

RICH CHOCOLATE MOUSSE

1 size 3 egg, separated
15g/½oz plain flour
25g/1oz sugar
150ml/¼ pint milk
1×15ml spoon/1 tablespoon brandy
50g/2oz plain chocolate, melted
15g/½oz gelatine
2×15ml spoons/2 tablespoons water
150ml/¼ pint double cream, whipped
vanilla essence
grated chocolate

Mix the egg yolk in a bowl with the flour and sugar. Mix the milk and brandy and pour into a pan. Bring almost to the boil and pour over the egg mixture, stirring all the time. Return to the pan and bring to the boil, still stirring, and cook for 2–3 minutes until quite thick. Stir in the melted chocolate. Cut a piece of greaseproof paper to fit the top of the pan and place over the chocolate custard. Leave to cool.

Soften the gelatine with the water in a small heatproof container. Stand the container in a pan of hot water and stir until dissolved. Whisk the egg whites until very stiff. Mix half the whipped cream with the chocolate custard and gelatine, and fold in the egg whites. Pour into a glass bowl or into individual glasses, and chill in a refrigerator until set.

Mix the rest of the cream with a little vanilla essence and use to decorate the top of the mousse, if liked, with the grated chocolate.

Raspberry Cream Brulée

375g/12oz fresh raspberries
150ml/¼ pint double cream
2×15ml spoons/2 tablespoons sugar
a few drops vanilla essence
4×15ml spoons/4 tablespoons soft brown sugar

Divide the raspberries between four heatproof ramekin dishes. Whip the cream with the sugar and vanilla essence until fairly stiff. Spoon over the top of the raspberries and push down the sides. Smooth the top with a spoon so that the surface is level. Spread the sugar over the top, making sure that no cream is exposed. Place under a hot grill and leave for a minute or two until the sugar begins to bubble. Remove from the heat and leave to cool. Chill for 1 hour before serving.

Summer Fruit Romanoff

250g/8oz fresh strawberries, sliced
½ fresh pineapple, peeled, cored and finely chopped
150ml/¼ pint whipping cream
2×15ml spoons/2 tablespoons sugar
2×15ml spoons/2 tablespoons kirsch
cocktail cherries, chopped

Mix together the strawberries and pineapple in a bowl. Whip the cream with the sugar and kirsch, and pour over the fruit. Chill for 1 hour. Just before serving, decorate the top with the cherries.

Melon Fruit Salad

1 honeydew melon
juice of 2 oranges
2 red skinned apples
1 green apple
1 fresh mango
175g/6oz strawberries, halved if large

Cut the top off the melon and scoop out the seeds. Cut out the flesh and cut into small pieces. Place in a bowl with the orange juice. Core and dice the apples and add to the melon in the bowl. Peel and stone the mango and add to the mixture with the strawberries. Mix the fruit together, pile back into the centre of the melon, and chill.
Serve with freshly whipped cream.

Orange and Kiwi Cream Flan

1×25cm/10 inch sponge flan base
5×15ml spoons/5 tablespoons orange marmalade
250g/8oz cream cheese **or** sieved cottage cheese
200ml/8fl oz double cream, lightly whipped
2 kiwi fruits, peeled and sliced
orange segments from 2 oranges

Place the sponge flan base on a large flat flan plate. Spread the marmalade all over the base. Beat the cream or cottage cheese until soft and creamy, and mix in the cream. Mix to a smooth, thick consistency and spread over the marmalade. Arrange the kiwi fruit and orange segments in an attractive pattern over the top.

Note Serves eight people

INDEX OF RECIPES